SOFTWARE ENGINEERING:
ANALYSIS AND DESIGN

THE McGRAW-HILL INTERNATIONAL SERIES IN SOFTWARE ENGINEERING

Consulting Editor

Professor D. Ince
The Open University

Forthcoming titles

Portable Modula-2 Programming
Software Documentation
SSADM — A User's Guide
Introduction to Formal Methods
Introduction to Compiling Techniques

SOFTWARE ENGINEERING: ANALYSIS AND DESIGN

Charles Easteal
University College London

Gordon Davies
The Open University

McGRAW-HILL BOOK COMPANY

London · New York · St Louis · San Francisco · Auckland · Bogotá · Guatamela
Hamburg · Lisbon · Madrid · Mexico · Montreal · New Delhi · Panama
Paris · San Juan · São Paulo · Singapore · Sydney · Tokyo · Toronto

Published by
McGRAW-HILL Book Company (UK) Limited
MAIDENHEAD · BERKSHIRE · ENGLAND

British Library Cataloguing in Publication Data
Easteal, Charles
  Software engineering: analysis and design. —
  (International software engineering series)
  1. Computer systems. Software. Development
  I. Title   II. Davies, Gordon   III. Open
  University   IV. Series
  005.1
  ISBN 0-07-707202-2

Library of Congress Cataloging-in-Publication Data
Easteal, Charles.
  Software engineering.
  (The McGraw-Hill international series in software
  engineering)
  Bibliography: p.
  Includes index.
  1. Software engineering.   I. Davies, Gordon.
II. Title.   III. Series.
QA76.758.E27   1989   005.1   89-2598
ISBN 0-07-707202-2

1234 WL 8909

Typeset by STYLESET LIMITED · WARMINSTER · WILTSHIRE

Printed and bound in Great Britain by Whitstable Litho Ltd

For David

CONTENTS

PREFACE

This book is based on material that was originally written for the Open University course *Fundamentals of Computing*; that course assumed no previous knowledge of computing whatsoever. However, the book is aimed more at students who have had some experience of computing, perhaps as a general introduction in a science or engineering degree, and who wish to gain further knowledge of how software is produced in the real world. Such students will not necessarily specialize in computer science while at college or university, but may well see their future employment as being in the computer industry.

The book deals with two phases of the Software Life Cycle. After two introductory chapters, three chapters are devoted to the analysis and specification of requirements; the final seven chapters deal with software design.

The book has been written with specific objectives for each of the main topics in mind. At the end of the chapters on analysis and specification of requirements the reader should have a general appreciation of the importance of this phase and, in particular, be able to:

1. Analyse a set of initial user requirements into four major categories, and be aware of the role that each category plays in software development.
2. Use one major technique for further detailed analysis of user requirements and employ three useful notations for recording the results of the analysis.
3. Compile a detailed specification of requirements to enable the design of the new software to commence.

On completing the chapters on software design the reader should have acquired an appreciation of the general principles involved and of the fundamental difficulties that are encountered. In particular, the reader should be able to:

1. Apply a particular and generally reliable design strategy to a representation of functional requirements in order to arrive at a first version of an initial design.
2. Refine the initial design by using design heuristics while appreciating the limitations of this procedure.

3. Convert each of the modules identified by 1 and 2 into algorithmic form and record the resulting detailed design by means of a natural language or graphical notation.
4. Design appropriate data structures for the algorithms designed in 3 to work upon.
5. Construct the appropriate documentation that terminates the design phase.

A number of exercises of varying difficulty are interspersed in the text and the reader is encouraged to spend a little time in attempting to answer these, as they are encountered, before studying the solutions which are included at the end of the book.

ACKNOWLEDGEMENTS

We would like to acknowledge the use of the following figures and quotations.

The following extracts from BS 6224:1987 are reproduced by permission of British Standards Institution. Complete copies of the Standard can be obtained from them at Linford Wood, Milton Keynes, Bucks., MK14 6LE, United Kingdom.

Figure 9.1b (BS Fig. 3); Figure 9.4 (BS Figs 5 and 6); Figure 9.9 (BS Fig. 7); Figure 9.11 (BS Fig. 8); Figure 9.7 (BS Fig. 10); Figures 9.2 and 9.3 (adaptation of BS Fig. 44b); Figure 9.5 (BS Fig. 45b); Figure 9.15 (adaptation of BS Fig. 47); Figure E13 (adaptation of BS Fig. 48).

The example in Section 7.2.3 (page 46) is adapted from J. C. Emery, *Organizational Planning and Control Systems*, Macmillan, London, 1969 (pages 18–19).

Figure 8.3 is adapted from G. J. Myers, *Reliable Software through Composite Design*, Van Nostrand Reinhold, Wokingham, 1975 (Figs 4.8 and 4.9).

The quotations on page 28 ('It is imprecise, wordy...and innuendo' and 'It is pidgin language...programming language)') are both taken from T. DeMarco, *Structured Analysis and System Specification*, Prentice-Hall, Englewood Cliffs, New Jersey, 1979 (pages 177 and 179, respectively).

The following are taken from E. Yourdon and L. L. Constantine, *Structural Design: Fundamentals of a Discipline of Computer Program and Systems Design*, Prentice-Hall, Englewood Cliffs, New Jersey, 1979: Quotation on page 57 ('A module is a lexically contiguous...identifier' from page 37); the adapted definition of functional cohesion on page 68 (from page 127); Figure 8.9 (similar to Figs 8.7, 8.8, 8.9, 8.10 from pages 153 and 154); Figure 8.19 (adaptation of Figs 10.5 and 10.6 from pages 193 and 196); Figure 8.20 (adaptation of Fig. 10.10 from page 200); Exercise 8.7 (adaptation of Figs 9.9a and 9.9b from pages 175 and 176).

The following are taken from M. Page-Jones, *The Practical Guide to Structured Systems Design*, 1st edn, Yourdon Press, New York, 1980: Figure 8.4 (adaptation of Fig. 6.3 from page 105); the quotation on page 85 ('A transaction...a new time slice' from pages 207–208).

Figure 11.1 is taken from R. S. Pressman, *Software Engineering: a Practitioner's Approach*, 1st edn, McGraw-Hill, London, 1982 (adaptation of a whole figure from 'Software Design Specification', pages 133–135).

1

INTRODUCTION

As a member of our target audience, you will almost certainly have written and run some computer programs. But it is important at this juncture to make three major points about your achievements:

(a) The programs that you wrote and handled were small. Although, no doubt, you were quite impressed with what could be achieved with a few lines of code, it is important to realize that many computer applications involve hundreds or even thousands of program statements. Indeed, an application consisting of a quarter of a million statements, say, is by no means unusual.

(b) In writing and running your programs you followed a detailed list of instructions that had been prepared by computer professionals, such as your lecturers or instructors. As a result, the instructions were free of ambiguity and left you in no doubt as to what you were required to do. In practice, of course, the vast majority of computer programs are not prepared for computer professionals. They are written by computer professionals for other types of professional, e.g., managers, engineers, accountants, etc. These individuals are generally known collectively, and perhaps rather loosely, as 'users'. And this is the term that will be used in referring to any organization or individual who requests or in any way sponsors, the development of computer software for practical purposes.

(c) Once the more obvious errors had been removed from a program that you had written, you were able to regard the job as finished. In the real world of computing, this is almost never the case. Just about every substantial piece of software that is released still contains errors. These will appear intermittently during the life of the program and will need to be corrected. As the working life of the program will often far exceed the life of the equipment on which it is first implemented, then it is clear that each program written represents a substantial future commitment for an organization's computer personnel.

Exercise 1.1 One reason has been given above (and another hinted at) as to why a program will need intermittent attention throughout its working life. Can you think of any other reasons why this must be so?

It should be apparent from the solution to the above exercise that the practical development and continuing efficient running of computer programs is a sizable on-going task, involving many people. Further, it is a multi-stage process in which the outputs of one stage are the inputs of the next. This sequence of stages has come to be known as the *software life cycle*.

THE SOFTWARE LIFE CYCLE

In order to discuss fully the activities involved in the life cycle, it is necessary to adopt a *model* of the cycle. The term 'model' may need some explanation. A model of something is merely a representation of that something that enables one to investigate its properties in a remote way. For instance, if the headlight on your motorcycle fails, even though you know that the bulb is working, you might be tempted to try and trace the wiring and hope to find a loose connection. You might be better employed, initially any way, in looking at the wiring diagram of the machine. You would then be studying something (the motorcycle wiring) remotely (in a warm kitchen rather than a cold garage) by means of a model (the wiring diagram). In the example case the model is constructed by means of a graphical notation, i.e., it is a picture. But often modelling is achieved in other ways. Natural language and mathematical symbols, for instance, are among the wide variety of notations that may be used for this purpose.

For example, consider the Lake District, a beautiful part of Nothern England. We can model the Lake District in two different ways, one using a graphical notation and one using natural language. An obvious graphical model would be an Ordnance Survey map; although photographs, provided that they concentrated on the scenery rather than bands of happy hill-walkers, would be an equally acceptable example. A guide-book would be a good instance of a natural language model, although you might suggest Wordsworth's poetry as being more in keeping with the spirit of the Lake District.

It is convenient for us to use a graphical notation to describe the software life cycle model and this is shown in Fig. 2.1.

You should note two basic points at this stage. First of all, the model that we are using is a graphical representation of a physical process. Not everyone will view the process in exactly the same way, so that you will find many variations on this model in textbooks. You should not allow this to confuse you, for the fundamental activities that

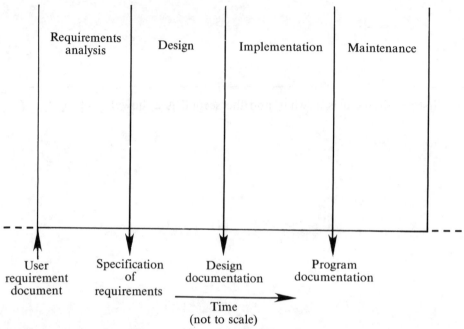

Figure 2.1 A simple model of the software life cycle.

are modelled will always be the same. The second point relates to the use of the adjective 'simple' in the figure title. You will probably infer that the life cycle may sometimes be more complex and, of course, you will be quite correct. But the reasons for the added complexity will not become clear until later in the book. As we have modelled the cycle it is apparent that it is a consecutive sequence of phases: requirements analysis, design, implementation and maintenance. The beginning and end of each phase is marked by the introduction or production of documents: the user requirement document, specification of requirements, design documentation and program documentation. The essential aspects of the simple model will now be described briefly.

2.1 USER REQUIREMENT DOCUMENT

The cycle commences with the receipt of this document by the body of individuals who are mandated to develop software for the user organization. The body may be an external contractor or a separate department of the user organization. The document should include statements of functional requirements. In other words, it should state clearly and unambiguously *what* is required of the software but not *how* this is to be achieved. For instance, a requirement might be that the proposed software should update a table. This is a perfectly acceptable expression of desired functionality. A statement which specifies the representation of the table in the computer is not, and it may be necessary to argue strongly for its exclusion. Just to reinforce this point, consider each of the following statements: is each one a 'what' or a 'how'?

Pop down to the newsagent and get me *The Times*.
Pop down to the take-away on your bike and get me a portion of the special fried rice.

The different nature of the purchases mentioned here is, of course, quite irrelevant. What is different is that the first statement is expressing a need; the second is expressing a need and giving explicit instructions as to the means of transportation to be used. Thus the first requirement is a 'what' and the second is a 'how'.

Usually, the user requirement document will also include some non-functional requirements. Most of these are acceptable and, indeed, may make life easier for the computer professionals of the development team later in the life cycle. A requirement that the average response to an enquiry of the database should not exceed five seconds, would come into the non-functional category. The distinction that we make between functional and non-functional requirements will become more clear in Sec. 3.1 of the next chapter.

2.2 REQUIREMENTS ANALYSIS

This represents a period of interaction between the user and the analyst, the latter being the computer professional assigned to work with the user during this phase. The original requirements are examined and tested for internal consistency. In other words, any contradictions or ambiguities among the requirements are discussed with the user until they are resolved to the satisfaction of both parties. The requirements are then refined until the user and the analyst are in complete agreement as to the expected detailed behaviour of the new software. It is important to remember that the majority of real-world programs that are written are replacements. They are intended to replace procedures that for various reasons have become obsolete. The procedures to be replaced may be manual or, increasingly, automated processes that no longer meet current needs. In these circumstances the behaviour of the existing system needs to be examined, for much of its existing functionality will need to be duplicated in the new system.

Exercise 2.1 How would you set about determining the behaviour of an existing procedure such as a group of clerical routines?

From the answer to Exercise 2.1 you will gather that requirements analysis can be a time-consuming exercise. Many man-months of effort may be necessary before the functionality of an existing system can be thoroughly understood. Finally, you should note that the emphasis of the work is still on what the software should do. The question of how it is to do it, is premature at this stage.

2.3 SPECIFICATION OF REQUIREMENTS

The production of this document ostensibly signals the end of the requirements analysis stage. In fact, the matter is not quite that simple but the reservation implied in the previous sentence need not concern us at the moment.

It is important to appreciate that the specification of requirements fulfils a dual role. On the one hand, it represents a form of contract between the user and the agency responsible for developing the new software. Consequently, the very substantial part of the specification that deals with the expected function must be written in a notation that is familiar to, and understandable by, the user. A notation based on English, or the appropriate natural language, suggests itself. On the other hand, it represents the starting point for the design phase and must therefore be easily interpreted by the software designer; a more formal graphical notation with less scope for ambiguity would seem more suitable. A notation that perfectly fulfils both roles has never been developed and probably never will be, although many attempts have been made. However, the combination of notations suggested in Chapter 3 enables a fairly good attempt to be made at achieving the ideal.

Of course there are some circumstances where a graphical notation is used publicly in preference to natural language. This is most likely to happen where there is a need to address people who have different natural languages, particularly if the message is to be put across without delay — hence the international convention for road signs and symbols on dashboards.

2.4 DESIGN

With the commencement of the design stage the attention of the software developers focuses on the question of how the user's requirements are to be implemented. This means that ideas on the structure of the programs and the data structures on which they will work are generated, and the best ideas are selected for further development. This is not as simple as it sounds. Consider a fairly simple design problem, the need to add three numbers. In how many ways could this be accomplished? (In other words: how many possible designs are there?)

The answer is four. If we let A, B, and C represent the numbers, we could add A and B, and then add the sum to C. Similarly, we could calculate $A + C$ and add it to B, or $B + C$ and add it to A. Finally, we could calculate $A + B + C$ in one fell swoop, thus making the fourth design.

But let us now take this design problem a little further and ask 'Roughly how many designs are there if we wish to add fifty numbers?'

If you arrived at the answer, 'quite a lot', then this would be acceptable; for the answer is 6.85×10^{81}. As a matter of interest, this is several magnitudes higher than the estimated number of atoms in the universe.

This gives some idea of the true magnitude of apparently simple design problems (Emery, 1969). In the case of software the number of distinct designs that could be considered is also immense — probably running into thousands for a small system; millions for a large one. This implies that a designer needs to use a design strategy in order that design may be accomplished in a reasonable time. The second feature that complicates the design process is the need to demonsrate that one design is superior to all others. This can only be achieved convincingly if the designer is able to measure competing designs against some appropriate 'yardstick'. This illustrates the need for design criteria, of which, unfortunately, there is no shortage.

The need for design criteria arises in many other situations. For example, what criteria do you think are used by the designer of motor cars?

Without knowing anything about this subject whatever, we presume that the design criteria include economy of running, certain aspects of road speed, safety, comfort, emission rates of noxious fumes, and so on.

The point that we wish to make is that comparing designs becomes increasingly difficult as the number of criteria increases. Hence the word 'unfortunately' in the sentence at the top of the page. The answer to Exercise 2.2 takes the matter a little further.

Exercise 2.2 What qualities, attributes or properties do you think should be taken into account in comparing software designs?

Detailed consideration of strategy and criteria must await a later chapter. For the moment it is sufficient to note that when the design stage is completed, the necessary documentation is available to enable the next phase, implementation, to proceed.

2.5 DESIGN DOCUMENTATION

The *design document* provides a channel of communication between the designer and the programmers who will convert the design into working computer programs. As such it will need to be expressed in a notation, or combination of notations, that leaves no shadow of doubt in the programmer's mind as to how the programs should function. Clearly, the notations need to be more formal at this stage and, consequently, less intelligible to the casual reader. Strictly speaking, there is no necessity for the user to understand this particular document so that its rather insular format need be of little concern.

However, it is sometimes the practice to issue other documents at this stage and these may have a wider readership. The *systems manual* is intended to provide a guide should changes need to be made to the system once it is in operation. It may need to be targeted, in part, at the non-expert user, particularly if the new software interfaces closely with clerical or manual routines. A *user manual* must be produced at some stage and the end of the design phase is often most appropriate. As its name implies, it is intended as the key reference to the system for the people who will actually use it. Finally, the user personnel need to learn how to use the system. Accordingly, a *user guide* or *tutorial* is often produced at this time.

2.6 IMPLEMENTATION

This phase involves a number of activities, of which writing and documenting programs is only one of the more important. It is commonly acknowledged that large software systems are best designed as a set of small, more easily handled pieces known as *modules*. As most of you will, by now, be used to writing computer programs, you will have encountered the concept of program modules before. The name that was given to them will vary, depending on the language you used.

Modules are equivalent to sub-routines, in the broadest sense, and there are specific programming language variants, e.g., procedure (Pascal and PL/1); function (Fortran); sub-program, section or paragraph (Cobol).

The testing and debugging of individual program modules is a critical activity, as is the *system test*. The latter is a full-scale attempt to ensure that all the program modules work together harmoniously and satisfy the user's requirements.

If the new software is a replacement for existing procedures, a possibility that we mentioned in Sec. 2.2, then the introduction into service of the new system may be regarded as being part of implementation. This is commonly referred to as *cut over* or *conversion*. It needs to be planned very carefully to ensure that the transition takes place smoothly and does not entail any loss or corruption of data.

Exercise 2.3 Can you think of one or two possible strategies for conversion?

2.7 PROGRAM DOCUMENTATION

A number of documents may be produced at this stage and various authorities have different views as to what they should be. Essential to the following maintenance phase are listings of the *source code* for the program modules and the *test log*, the latter being an account of the test procedures to which the modules have been subjected, and the results obtained. Also emerging from implementation may be updated versions of documents that originated earlier in the cycle. For instance, it may have been necessary to modify the user and systems manuals and issue new versions.

2.8 MAINTENANCE

In Chapter 1 we noted that software will continue to receive attention throughout its working life and in Exercise 1.2 we examined the reasons why this should be so. An interesting statistic is provided by a number of practitioners and researchers in the subject. They seem to be largely in agreement that maintenance, on average, accounts for about 70 per cent of the total life-cycle costs of a piece of software. In other words, more than twice as much is spent on changing it as on building it in the first place. It is not surprising, therefore, that in recent years considerable effort has been devoted to reducing the costs incurred in maintaining software. Much work has been done on improving documentation techniques and providing better *software tools* for the developers. Software tools are computer programs that are intended to improve the efficiency of analysts, designers and programmers. They include text editors, arguably the most important, and packages to assist with debugging, testing, and so on. However, it has been realized that one of the best ways to check excessive maintenance costs is to accept that maintenance will always be necessary, and design with this fact in mind. In terms of Exercise 2.2, maintainability should be given a higher weighting as a design criterion, at the expense of some of the other properties mentioned. Design methods have been developed that tend to produce systems that are highly maintainable and we look at some of these later in the book.

2.9 CONCLUSION

In concluding the above brief account of the simple model of the software life cycle, there are four major points to be made:

(a) The way that we have displayed and described the life cycle has probably tempted you to believe that progress through the cycle is orderly and fundamentally linear. It is not. In fact, if we re-draw the life-cycle diagram and concentrate on information flows, then our graphical model begins to look like Fig. 2.2. The point is that,

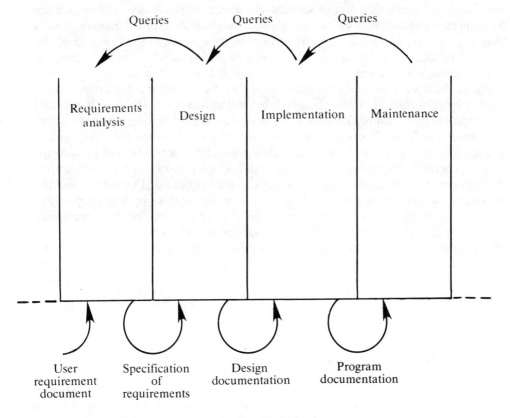

Figure 2.2 Information flows and the software life cycle.

inevitably, there is a need to refer back to earlier phases when later phases are under way. For instance, during implementation a programmer may encounter a feature that needs clarification by a designer. The designer may recognize that a design error has been made, and advise the programmer accordingly. Equally, he may decide that the specification is unclear and refer the matter back even further in the cycle for more analysis. So, while the cycle progresses steadily forward, there are constant but temporary re-visitations to earlier activities.

(b) It is necessary to bear in mind that the programs produced during implementation must be consistent with the original user requirements. The requirements, originally expressed in natural language, have undergone a sequence of transformations into specialist notations and eventually into program code. Each transformation must be checked to ensure that correctness and consistency is maintained, an activity that is commonly known as *validation*. One substantial validation activity is program testing, the painstaking use of test data to ensure as far as possible that each path through each module delivers the correct result. However, there is more to it than that, for the transformations at previous stages have to be checked out through time-consuming manual examination. A number of procedures are used by computer professionals to formalize manual validation activities and make them more effective. A large amount of research activity is devoted to validation with the expectation that it will ultimately become possible to prove mathematically that a program meets the original requirements correctly. Thus, the need for manual validation and program testing will be removed. The day will come, no doubt, when this will largely be achieved, but it is not yet here.

(c) We have already encountered the question of cost in the context of the proportion of total life-cycle costs that are absorbed by maintenance on the one hand, and development (i.e., requirements analysis, design and implementation) on the other. It is always difficult to analyse the allocation of costs between the development phases, for different models of the life cycle are used by different people. However, it is now generally accepted that the analysis and design phases can account for up to 50 per cent of development costs. Coding accounts for about 15 per cent and the testing phase takes 35 per cent. While there may be fluctuations in these proportions from project to project, the figures generally indicate that, in cost terms, programming is a much less significant activity than analysis and design.

(d) You will have noted that the simple model of the life cycle (Fig. 2.1) indicates with a vertical line that the maintenance phase ultimately terminates. You may have wondered why. The answer is that after some years of operation the software is so obsolete that it is not worth continuing to maintain it; and then the whole cycle begins again.

2.10 SUMMARY

In this chapter we have introduced the concept of the software life cycle and explained very briefly the activities involved in each phase. We have also noted the key documents associated with the demarcation of the phases. The following chapters are concerned with the activities of requirements analysis and the preparation of the specification of requirements. Design receives detailed consideration in the later chapters of the book.

REFERENCE

Emery, J. C. (1969) *Organizational Planning and Control Systems*, Macmillan, London.

3

REQUIREMENT ANALYSIS

In the previous chapter we described the specification of requirements, which terminates the analysis phase, as 'a form of contract between the user and the agency responsible for developing the new software'. We intend this to be interpreted as a formal agreement on the detailed behaviour of the software rather than as invoking any financial considerations. Thus, in order to represent the agreed behaviour, we need to adopt a notation that is intelligible to the user. It needs to be interpretable by the designer also for, as you will recall, the specification provides the major input to the design stage. This notation must be based on a *view*.

The concept of a view is a very important but simple one in computing. All it means is that in observing a system of any type there are features or qualities possessed by the system which express its basic nature. However, different people with different interests will not necessarily be interested in the same features. For example, the view of the system that we know as a school, as seen by a teacher, is rather different from the view taken by the pupils. The view of a rapid-transit railway system, as seen by the traffic manager say, will almost certainly differ from the view taken by the chief engineer. To the former it may be seen as packets of people encased in metal hurtling over or under the ground; to the latter it is an assemblage of rolling stock, track, signalling systems, workshops, etc. This is not to say, of course, that either is unaware of the other's interests. It is just that the variables of immediate concern to each are different.

Exercise 3.1 What views of a petrol filling station might be taken by (a) a motorist and (b) the owner of a fast food chain?

In the same way that different views may be taken of a school, rapid-transit railway system or a filling station, different views may be taken of an information system. In this chapter we adopt a particular, and very popular, view and introduce appropriate notations for recording and display. However, before we attempt that task, we shall see that considerable progress can be made if we make our first act of analysis a critical examination of the user requirement document.

3.1 PRELIMINARY ANALYSIS OF USER REQUIREMENT DOCUMENT

The user requirement document may be brief. In fact, if the function of the software is to be simple and straightforward, then little more than a title may be required. A routine to calculate square roots of numbers could well come into this category. But on the whole, life is not that simple and the user requirement will consist of a number of statements. Consider, for example, Fig. 3.1.

Purchase Commitments System

A software package is to be developed to meet the following requirements:

   (a) Purchase order information is to be accepted as input.

   (b) Records are to be ordered on *supplier number* and organized sequentially.

   (c) Purchase commitments records are to be maintained for one, two and three months ahead.

   (d) The size of the database should be no larger than 4 megabytes.

   (e) The system should permit easy and efficient maintenance.

   (f) Control information must be supplied regularly to management.

   (g) All software must comply with corporate standards.

Figure 3.1 User requirements for a purchase commitments system.

A purchase commitments system is used by companies to show future money obligations arising from orders for goods that have been placed with outside suppliers. Usually, a company's accountants like to see the corresponding outflow of cash as it is scheduled to occur in one month, two months, etc. With that background we can examine the various statements made by the user and determine their relevance to the task ahead, i.e., building some new software to support the purchase commitments function.

3.1.1 Functional requirements

Of all the user requirements the most critical at this stage are those which describe the desired functionality of the new software. In other words, we are interested in statements that tell us what is expected of the system in behavioural terms. In particular, we need to know what information is to be input to the software and what outputs are required. If we examine statement (a) of Fig. 3.1 we can see that this is clearly a functional requirement, not a particularly useful one, but a functional requirement, nevertheless. For it is telling us, in very general terms, what type of information is to provide input to the new software.

Exercise 3.2 Which other statements in Fig. 3.1 do you regard as functional requirements?

There are still some statements unaccounted for. But they all have some role in the software development process and we must now categorize them and consider what this role will be.

3.1.2 Non-functional requirements

These are, in effect, constraints on the software designer. They have the effect of limiting choice. So that many ostensibly possible designs are removed and do not have to be assessed. They, thus, play a valuable role.

Non-functional requirements (or constraints, as we shall sometimes refer to them) are frequently concerned with hardware and software. For instance, a user requirement statement might be: 'the package is to be implemented on the Slime 43'. The user is telling the designer that this is the marque of computer that he uses. Consequently, there is no point in designing and implementing a system that is intended to run on an IBM PC or a VAX 11/750. Similarly, a statement to the effect that the package is to be implemented in Fortran 77 indicates, most probably, that all of the existing programs are written in this language, and that the user is quite happy with them and has no intention of allowing software written in Basic, Cobol or Pascal through the door.

Other constraints relate to time or money. A user may need to have the software available by a certain date, or may have a cost ceiling in mind that should not be exceeded. Hence, there is little point in designing a system that is so complex that it stands no chance of meeting the deadline, or is so expensive that the user cannot meet the cost without exceeding the budget.

No doubt you will have noted the intrusion of the word *designer* into the second paragraph of this section. This gives a clue as to where non-functional requirements have a role to play. For they are allowed to bypass requirements analysis and feed directly into the design phase.

Exercise 3.3 Which statements in Fig. 3.1 do you regard as relating to non-functional requirements?

3.1.3 Design objectives

From the solutions to Exercises 3.2 and 3.3 you will see that we have still not accounted for all of the user requirement statements for the purchase commitments software. You will rightly suspect, therefore, that there is at least one other category into which statements might fall. You will recall that in Sec. 2.4 we introduced the idea of design criteria, the properties or attributes of software that enable designs to be compared. We expanded on this idea in Exercise 2.2 and mentioned the systems designer's art of 'trading off'. Regrettably, we now have to complicate these simple concepts. Once the designer appreciates the relative importance that the user places on these properties, then he or she can be said to have one or more design objectives. For instance, if the user makes security the first priority, then the design objective becomes very clear, and may be expressed as follows: 'select the design that maximizes security, subject to compliance with any constraints, and which makes adequate provision for maintainability, robustness, reliability, etc.'. This takes due note of the user's preference but clearly eliminates a highly secure design that will cost three times the user's computing budget for the decade to implement, and is expected to break down every five minutes. One way in which the user may convey his or her attitude towards design objectives may be via the user requirement document. And here, <u>it is important to appreciate the distinction</u> between *design objectives* and *non-functional requirements*. The latter eliminate designs; the former offer advice on how to distinguish between designs that in other respects are rather similar.

Exercise 3.4 Are there any design objectives among the statements in Fig. 3.1?

3.1.4 Design decisions

There is one statement left, (b). This is a rather unwelcome intruder but, nevertheless, it is the type of statement that is often encountered, particularly if the user is relatively experienced in the use of computing techniques. Basically, in specifying the type of file organization that is wanted, the user is taking a design decision prematurely. In a nutshell, the wrong person is taking the wrong decision at the wrong time and, for all we know at this stage, sowing the seeds for future disaster. Why does the user do it? Probably because he or she has had experience of similarly organized files in the past and has always found them satisfactory. However, there are many other ways of organizing files and in this case, when requirements analysis is completed and design is well under way, a far better solution may present itself. In general, an attempt by anyone to introduce the topic of how behaviour is to be achieved, rather than what behaviour is desired, is to be strongly deprecated at this stage. When the user is the culprit there is only one course open to the analyst, and that is to try and persuade the user to withdraw the statement. If this fails, there is no option but to accept the decision with good grace. In which case the maverick design decision must be re-interpreted as a non-functional requirement. It will thus fulfil the role of eliminating many possible designs including, life being what it is, some of the best.

We can now summarize our analysis of the requirements for the purchase commitments system by listing the statements that come into each category. We concluded that (a), (c) and (f) are functional, and (d) and (g) non-functional requirements; (e) is a design objective; (b) is a design decision.

3.1.5 Methodology

We have now recognized four classes into which requirements statements may be grouped. The need now is for a formal procedure by means of which we can separate and dispatch them in accordance with the main activities of the life cycle. There are several approaches to this and one of them is illustrated in Fig. 3.2. No claim is made for the superiority of this approach over any other. But it has been found to work and seems to have an intrinsic logic that appeals to many.

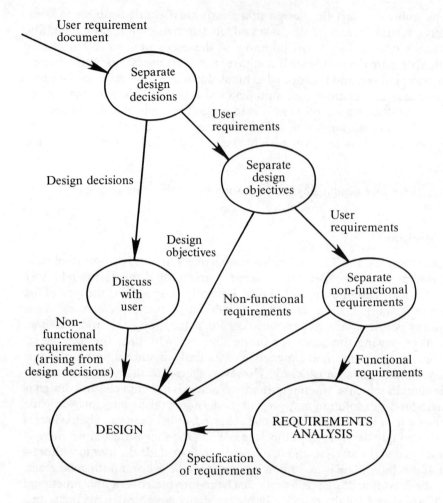

Figure 3.2 Analysis of the User requirement document.

We have illustrated the procedure by means of a simple chart. The small circles represent selection processes; the large circles represent stages of the life cycle. The chart should be interpreted as follows.

User requirement document We show the original document expressing the user requirements entering the first process in the preliminary analysis procedure.

Separation of design decisions At this point, design decisions are separated out and referred back to the user. If the user can be persuaded to withdraw them, all well and good. If not, the design decisions are confirmed and from this point on are regarded as constraints on the design process, i.e., non-functional requirements. As such, they have no part to play in requirements analysis. So, bypassing this phase they are introduced directly into design.

Separation of design objectives The remaining statements are analysed and any design objectives are extracted. These also are channelled into the design phase.

Separation of non-functional requirements There are only two categories remaining: functional and non-functional requirements. The latter are extracted and, once again, directed into the design phase.

Requirements analysis The remaining statements, representing true functional requirements, become the trigger that initiates requirements analysis proper.

Specification of requirements In Sec. 2.3 we dealt briefly with the role of this document and we shall have more to say later. However, it is worth making a further point now. Figure 3.2 shows three independent flows of information, in addition to the specification of requirements, making their way to design. They are non-functional requirements (arising from former design decisions), design objectives and true non-functional requirements. It is technically safer and administratively more convenient to formalize the channel by which they are communicated to the designers. An eminently suitable channel exists, of course. It is the specification of requirements. And so, the practice is frequently encountered whereby this document incorporates sections dealing with the three information flows mentioned above.

Exercise 3.5 Figure 3.3 is a user requirement document for wind-tunnel-monitoring software. It lists the requirements for a program that will monitor pressure readings from objects placed in a wind tunnel for aerodynamic testing. Categorize the requirements in accordance with the recommended procedure outlined above.

3.1.6 Summary

We have examined the nature of the types of user requirement commonly encountered and recommended a procedure for analysing user requirement documents. For the moment we can mentally discard three of the categories. However, the remaining category represents prime input to the requirements analysis stage and must receive our full attention. First let us remind you of which of the requirements listed for the purchase commitments system in Fig. 3.1 are input to requirements analysis.

The category that we are interested in is the functional requirements and for the purchase commitments system these are: (a) purchase order information is to be accepted as input; (c) purchase commitment records are to be maintained for one, two and three months ahead; (f) control information must be supplied regularly to management.

From these three functional requirements we receive a broad idea of the desired functionality. However, a number of questions are left hanging in the air. What does purchase order information consist of? How many commitment records might there be at any time? What is control information anyway? These questions and many more need to be answered, and the answers recorded, during the subsequent requirements analysis phase. The methods whereby we obtain answers have been dealt with in the

---

Requirement Document

Wind-tunnel Monitor

1. The program is to monitor pressure readings from strain gauges placed on objects held in a wind tunnel.

2. The program must be written in the assembly language of the computer used (Motorola M68000).

3. Signals received by the computer will come from a serial line. They will be of the form:

pressure gauge no.	pressure
5 bits	11 bits

   Each signal will be in EBCDIC format and will represent a pressure reading for 1 second.

4. The program will be no larger than 2600 bytes.

5. A general aim in the design of the program is to minimize the amount of main memory used.

6. The program will monitor the pressure readings over a period of time of no longer than 24 hours.

7. Before a wind-tunnel experiment starts the tunnel operator must provide the program with the following items of data:

   7.1 A symbolic name for each pressure point and the number of the pressure gauge associated with that point.

   7.2 The period over which a pressure average is to be taken (AVERAGEPERIOD). This should not be less than 5 seconds or more than 30 minutes.

8. At the end of the wind-tunnel experiment the program must produce, for each pressure gauge, a report. This must consist of:

   8.1 The name of the pressure point.

   8.2 A list of pressure averages over AVERAGEPERIOD for the duration of the experiment.

9. The program must consist of three procedures:

   9.1 A procedure which deals with the input and processing of data.

   9.2 A procedure which deals with the interaction between the wind-tunnel operator and the program.

   9.3 A procedure which produces the average summaries.

Figure 3.3 User requirement document for a wind tunnel monitoring program.

solution to Exercise 2.1. We now have to give some attention to the recording aspect, bearing in mind the need to use appropriate notations.

The question of notation is an important one as there are two categories of individual who need to be able to interpret the record of detailed requirements that we make. Remember we are now talking about the output from requirements analysis, i.e., the specification of requirements, and this is aimed at both the *user* and the *designer* so that the notations we use must be acceptable to both. We must now introduce these notations along with any customs or regulations that govern their use.

3.2 DATAFLOW ANALYSIS

3.2.1 Introduction

At the beginning of this chapter we made the point that the choice of notations that we make depends on the view that we take of information systems. Our view will be a simple one based on flows of information. We will find that it is as convenient for us to adopt this view as it is for a plumber to view a domestic central heating system as flows of water.

The flows we are interested in range from simple electronic signals (as in the case of the input to the wind-tunnel monitor, Fig. 3.3) to complex documents (as in the case of the input to the purchase commitments system, Fig. 3.1). The physical nature of the flows, at this stage, is irrelevant, but their fate is certain. Every flow of information that enters the system will either enter a process and be changed to another flow, or be stored either temporarily or with a greater degree of permanence, or leave the system.

If we look back at the user requirement document, Fig. 3.1, we can determine what information flows will enter the purchase commitment system. At this stage, the only one that we know positively will exist is the flow of purchase order information. Other flows may become apparent when we become more deeply involved in requirements analysis.

Exercise 3.6 What information flows will enter the wind-tunnel monitoring software, according to the user requirement document, Fig. 3.3?

3.2.2 Dataflow analysis

The technique involves, therefore, the identification of the three basic elements involved in the information system, namely *flows, processes* (although, to avoid confusion with another use of the word, *transforms* is a better term to use) and *stores*. In the case of the latter term, *files* is also used, and we will therefore use both. The elements are recorded and their inter-relationships are shown by means of a graphical notation known formally as a *dataflow diagram*, casually as a *DFD* and irreverently as a *bubble chart*. Now, there is no officially accepted set of symbols for displaying a dataflow diagram. So we shall use a set proposed by a very active and persuasive advocate of the dataflow approach (DeMarco, 1979). There are only four mandatory symbols involved and these are all incorporated in Fig. 3.4.

3.2.3 Dataflow diagram notation

First, you will have noted that, included in Fig. 3.4, there are two circles labelled T1 and T2. (As this diagram is for illustrative purposes only, we have used symbolic names.) The circles represent transforms and, in practice, they each would carry a short, pithy but indicative name that would convey some idea as to the nature of the transformation within. Also included in the diagram there are no less than five arrows: I1, I2, I3, I4 and I5. Each of these represents a flow of information and the arrow-head indicates the direction of flow. So we can see that I3, say, is a flow of information that is an output of T1 and an input to T2. You will note that T1 has two inputs, I1 and I2, and these are transformed by T1 into the information flow, I3. T2 has the one input (I3) and transforms this into two different flows (I4 and I5) which are its outputs. Once again, the flows would, in practice, each be labelled with a short descriptive name. The arrow indicating flow I2 emanates from a short horizontal line labelled F1. This symbol represents a store or file and the diagram indicates that I2 is stored within the system. (This begs the question as to how I2 arrived in the store in the first place but as we are merely demonstrating the use of the symbols we will not persist with this line of enquiry.)

There is one other file recorded in Fig. 3.4; it is F2 and this clearly stores the components of the flow I5. As before, F1 and F2 would, in practice, be short descriptive names. The only symbol that we have not mentioned is the square, of which there are two on the diagram. S1 is a source. That is, it represents the place of origin of the flow, I1. S2 is a sink and represents the destination of flow I4. Although, at first sight the roles of S1 and S2 seem to be completely different, they do in fact have a common purpose. They delimit the system. In other words, they place a boundary around the system that is being analysed. This boundary is easily constructed in the following way: draw a line that intersects each flow from a source and each flow into a sink, ensuring that all transforms and files are enclosed. This has been done for Fig. 3.4, the result being displayed in Fig. 3.5.

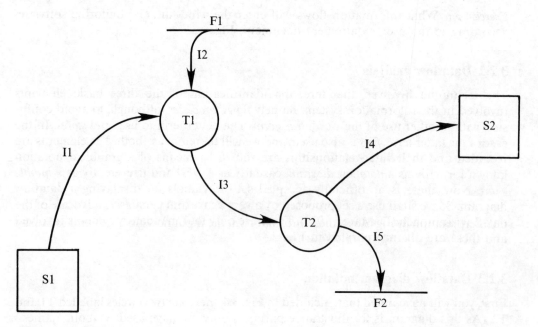

Figure 3.4 A fragment of a dataflow diagram using the DeMarco convention.

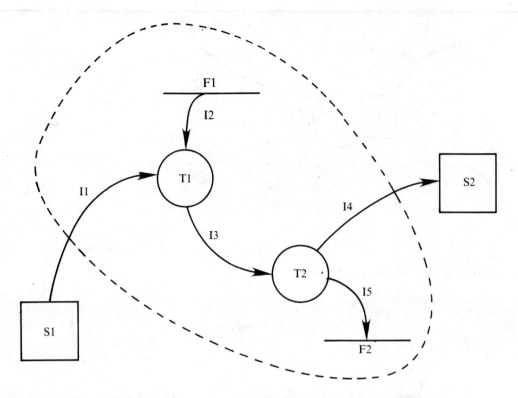

Figure 3.5 The dataflow diagram of Fig. 3.4 with the system boundary superimposed.

The implication for the analyst is that whatever happens within S1 and S2 (maybe separate departments of an organization) is none of his or her business. The analyst's hands will be full enough dealing with the complexities of T1, T2, I1, I2, I3, I4, I5, F1 and F2. A final point: some analysts like to use a further development of the notation. This is illustrated in Fig. 3.6.

The diagram includes two new symbols:

* meaning AND, i.e., a conjunction of information flows

+ meaning OR, i.e., a disjunction of information flows

The interpretation of Fig. 3.6 is, therefore, that both the input flows to T4, I5 and I6 must be present. And that one or other of the output flows, I7 or I8 (but not both), will result. DeMarco's view is that this convention should be used sparingly, if at all — a view with which the authors of this book wholeheartedly agree. Nevertheless, it is important that you should understand the meaning of this symbolism even if you manage to avoid using it yourself.

Exercise 3.7 What is your interpretation of Fig. 3.7?

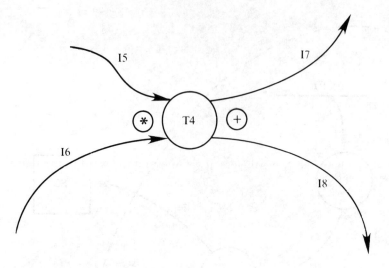

Figure 3.6 Procedural annotation of DFDs (1).

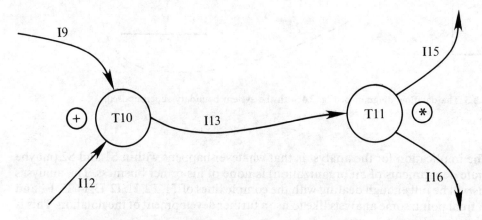

Figure 3.7 Procedural annotation of DFDs (2).

3.2.4 Summary

In Sec. 3.2 we have introduced a convenient way of viewing systems that is based on the concept of information flow. We have also seen that information flows, with their associated transforms and stores, may be modelled by a very simple notation known as the dataflow diagram. However, as we are sure you will agree, it is one thing to know of a technique, but quite another to be able to apply it. So Sec. 3.3 will be devoted to using DFDs. Do not be too surprised if the overall attack bears some similarity to the ideas of programming strategy that you have already been taught. By the way, you will probably have realized that we used a simplified form of DFD to illustrate the analysis of user requirements, Fig. 3.2.

3.3 THE PRACTICAL APPROACH

3.3.1 Introduction

It is alleged that an infamous character once said: 'Every time I hear the word 'culture', I reach for my gun' — or words to that effect. Without offering support for this sentiment or sympathy for the character, the writers have similar feelings towards the word 'structured'. It does seem that anyone who believes that he or she has a contribution to make in virtually any field, feels obliged to bring the word in somewhere to lend credibility to whatever views are being advanced. Nevertheless, if we interpret the word in the sense that it is used in connection with computer programming, i.e., to take a top-down approach to problem solving, then it seems sensible for requirements analysis to be pursued in the same way. This can be justified quite simply. Almost by definition, detailed procedures change more rapidly than major activities. In the days when the bottom-up approach to requirements analysis was the norm, many analysts became so bogged down in recording ever-changing detail that they never reached the position of being able to tackle the higher, and thus more important, requirements. It is now appreciated that it is far better to record the more stable upper levels and defer the assessment of the more volatile lower reaches until later. Thus, despite our previously stated misgivings about the word, we are going to set about analysis in a structured fashion.

3.3.2 Structured analysis

Level 0 One big advantage of this approach is that the first move that we make is an easy one. We view the whole system as one large transform (which indeed it is), show the inputs arriving from sources and outputs leaving for sinks, and the job is done. What we have constructed is commonly known as the level 0 dataflow diagram. On the basis of the user requirement we can construct such a diagram for the purchase commitments system, and this is shown as Fig. 3.8.

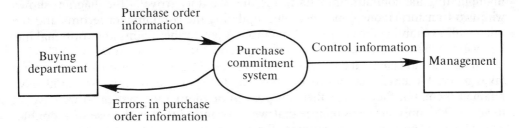

Figure 3.8 Level 0 dataflow diagram for the purchase commitments system.

This diagram is based almost entirely on the user requirement document. The only evidence of bringing our imagination into play is the labelling of the source of the purchase order information as the Buying Department. In practice, of course, even this tentative leap would almost certainly be unnecessary. Even if we did not know already, a simple enquiry would soon identify the source of purchase order information for us. The other feature not mentioned in the user requirement document is the information flow labelled 'Errors in purchase order information'. Its inclusion is not due to imagination but to hard experience. Input information always contains errors which must be returned to the source for correction.

Finally, what do we do about the Buying Department procedures that give rise to the purchase order information? A brief reprise of Sec. 3.2.3 indicates that the answer is *nothing*. The Buying Department is a source and thus outside the system boundary. Management is similarly out of bounds because of its status as a sink.

Exercise 3.8 Draw the level 0 dataflow diagram for the wind-tunnel monitoring system.

Level 1 The level 0 diagram has the considerable merit of getting us started along the dataflow road by causing us to assemble our knowledge in the correct format with little intellectual effort. But it tells us little that is new. In order to record what is new, we have to refine or, colloquially, explode the original transform into several subsidiary transforms with linking, and more detailed, information flows. It is at this point that those of you who have been taught the programming technique of top-down design and step-wise refinement should remember that technique, for we are using the same type of step-wise refinement that you encountered then. This explosion leads to the development of the level 1 DFD. If the user requirement document is very detailed we may be able to sketch the level 1 DFD without more ado. If it is rather vague and unspecific, like the purchase commitment document, then some fact-finding may be called for. Even so, there is probably enough information in the purchase commitment document to enable us to take a stab at a first level explosion. The result is illustrated in Fig. 3.9.

The rationale for this is as follows. Statement (c) of Fig. 3.1 indicates that records are to be maintained for one, two and three months ahead. Records imply the presence of a file, which we have included and named the commitment file. Further, it seems likely that the control information mentioned in statement (f) will be produced by periodically manipulating the commitment data in the file. We thus arrive at the diagram shown with two transforms: one concerned with updating the commitment records and the other with assembling the control information. A few further points are worth making. You will see that we have now associated a numerical ID with each transform. This is a useful measure to take for it enables us to keep track of transforms as further refinement takes place. We have abandoned the symbols for source and sink. We could have retained them, but they served their purpose in delimiting the system so we have let them go. The only new symbolism that we have introduced is the use of a double-headed arrow between the commitment file and transform 1. This indicates a two-way flow between the file and the transform. We could just as easily, and legally, have used two arrows pointing in opposite directions, but it reduces the clutter on the diagram to use just one. A final point: the inputs and outputs to the level 1 diagram are the same as those for the level 0 transform. A check that this is so is an important aspect of determining the internal consistency of a set of DFDs.

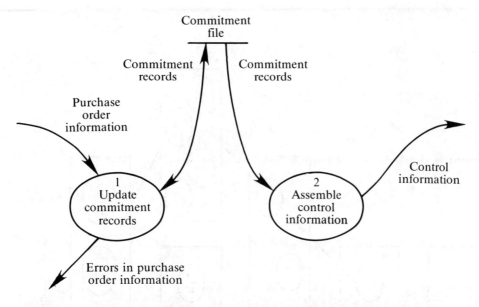

Figure 3.9 Level 1 dataflow diagram for the purchase commitments system.

Exercise 3.9 Try and develop a level 1 DFD for the wind-tunnel monitoring software. (This is quite a difficult exercise if you have never attempted the step-wise refinement of DFDs before, so set yourself a time limit of half an hour or so.)

Levels 2, 3, etc. The transforms of Fig. 3.9 are still not particularly informative so the next move is to refine them both further. We would then have two more diagrams. One would be a further refinement of transform 1 and would include transforms 1.1, 1.2, 1.3, etc. The other would be a refinement of transform 2 incorporating transforms 2.1, 2.2, 2.3, and so on. And so the process would go on, each transform at a particular level being exploded to a level below. Of course, at some point refinement has to stop. Transforms that we cannot or do not wish to refine further are called *primitive transforms* and some guidance in identifying them is offered in the next section. After we have completed our analysis we would have what is termed a *levelled set* of DFDs. A diagrammatic representation of how this set might appear is shown in Fig. 3.10. We have included only transforms (with their IDs) in the diagram. Representations of dataflows, data files and labels generally, have been omitted for clarity.

Although guidance in the identification of primitives is given in the next section, we can now identify the primitives of Fig. 3.10. The primitive transforms are those that are not exploded or refined any further. Although we can see that the refinement extends to level 4, as early as level 2 some primitives had been identified, namely 1.1 and 2.1. At level 3, 1.2.1, 1.2.2, 1.3.1, 1.3.2, 2.2.1, 2.2.2 and 2.2.4 were found to be primitive. And at level 4, 1.2.3.1, 1.2.3.2, 2.2.3.1 and 2.2.3.2 were similarly found to be primitive.

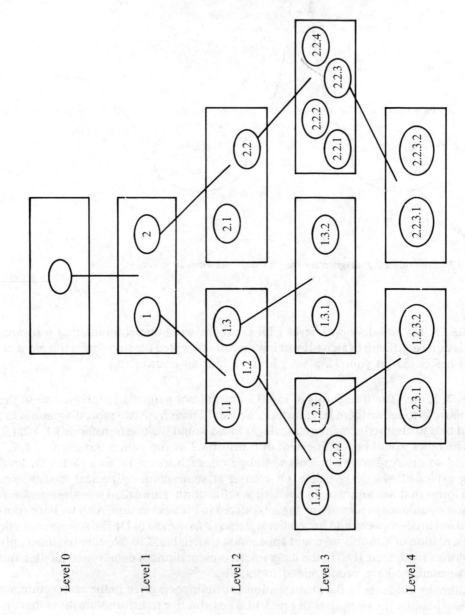

Figure 3.10 A possible levelled set of DFDs for the purchase commitments system.

Level 0

Level 1

Level 2

Level 3

Level 4

Identifying primitives The point at which a transform should be declared primitive and further refinement stopped is sometimes evident and sometimes not. DeMarco (1979) in his estimable book gives three guidelines which, for a first-time user, are as good as any. They are:

(a) Cease refinement of a transform when it can be completely specified on one page. (This requires some knowledge of transform specification techniques which we have not yet encountered, so we will pass on without comment.)
(b) Continue refining until all transforms have a single input flow and a single output flow. DeMarco points out, however, that frequently there will be transforms that cannot be refined to this stage.
(c) Stop refinement when the ratio of input flows to output flows is one-to-many or many-to-one. A many-to-many ratio is a sign that refinement is incomplete.

DeMarco states that all three can be useful but his own preference seems to be for method (a). But he notes that it tends to be an iterative approach, for it is only when you try to specify a primitive within the constraints of one page that you may realize it is not a primitive after all and further refinement is advised.

3.3.3 Summary

Albeit briefly, we have examined the practical aspects of dataflow analysis and now some words of caution are due. Firstly, although the dataflow diagram is a useful and simple notation to use, it has one major drawback. As the number of transforms on a diagram increases then so does its incomprehensibility. The upper limit seems to be about six transforms. So it seems to make good sense to try and observe this limit whenever possible. This is not to say that you should indulge in contorted refinement merely to play the numbers game. But it is most definitely to say that if you explode a transform into twenty-three primitives, then it is worth checking your work. If the laws of nature mean anything at all, then you have almost certainly missed out an interim level.

Throughout Secs 3.2 and 3.3 the user has received barely a mention. But he or she is not forgotten, for every level of refinement needs to be checked out with the user. After all, the levelled set of DFDs express the overall functionality of the software that the user is expecting to receive, and is part of that 'contract' that we mentioned much earlier. A final reminder: at each level of refinement the analyst must check rigorously that the inputs to and outputs from the exploded transform match exactly with those of the next level DFD. In the absence of any formal method of proving validity this is the best that can be done.

3.4 SUPPLEMENTARY NOTATIONS

The levelled set of dataflow diagrams leaves two major questions unanswered. What really goes on inside the primitive transforms? and What do the information flows and the files consist of? Unless we can record the answers to those questions our specification of requirements is sadly incomplete.

Exercise 3.10 Why do we not need a means of recording the inner behaviour of non-primitive transforms?

Let us now look at some appropriate notations for attempting this task.

3.4.1 Specification of primitive transforms

We are still in pursuit of an acceptable combination of clarity and formality, and these desirable properties will naturally limit the choice of notations for preparing *mini-specs*, as specifications for primitive transforms are frequently called. The most commonly suggested options are

natural language

flowcharts (using a standard convention)

decision tables

decision trees

structured English

Of these, natural language is, superficially, the most attractive and has a number of adherents. However, it has a number of weaknesses. DeMarco (1979) is not overstating the case when he claims of English (or any natural language) that 'It is imprecise, wordy, redundant, and full of implications, connotations, and innuendo.' Although, natural language will always have its uses it is unwise to depend on it as the prime notation for mini-specs. Flowcharts, of course, are commonly used but their popularity is on the wane. The point is that flowchart-based specifications are not easily transformed into designs and programs when the implementation language is a modern high-level one such as Pascal or one of its derivatives. Decision tables come highly recommended and have the merit of being, arguably, the most user-friendly of the specification techniques. They have the disadvantage of not being able to represent looping or repetition unless they are specially adapted, at which point their clarity diminishes, therefore it is not proposed to discuss them further at this stage. The idea of using decision trees for mini-specs is, in the writers' opinion, quite absurd. For a start, the notation referred to in this context is not a decision tree at all but a re-formatted decision table. As such it brings nothing new to the specification process. We are left, having completed a semi-hatchet job on the opposition, with structured English (despite the occurrence of that word again) as our main specification tool.

Structured English 'It is a pidgin language in that it uses the vocabulary of one language (i.e., English) and the overall syntax of another (i.e., a structured programming language)' (DeMarco, 1979). DeMarco is, in fact, quoting from a conference paper where the definition was applied to something else. But he points out, quite correctly, that the statement is equally applicable to structured English. The vocabulary of structured English is limited as far as possible to the following:

(a) Imperative English language verbs.

(b) Terms defined in the data dictionary. (We will consider data dictionaries in Sec. 3.4.2. For the moment, accept that we are referring to the names of information flows, stored information and their components.)

(c) Certain reserved words that are used to help formulate the internal logic of transforms.

It is permissible to relax the vocabulary rules if necessary. This is likely to be the case if certain nuances of meaning cannot be conveyed within the strict framework above. The syntax is limited to:

(a) Simple sentences.
(b) Decision constructs, e.g., if-then-else, case-of.
(c) Repetition constructs, e.g., do-while, repeat-until.

As there are no presentational standards to be observed (other than those adopted by individual organizations) you will encounter structured English mini-specs in many formats. Figure 3.11 shows two examples.

PROCESS ID:AC 3.1.5	PROCESS NAME: Calculate Depreciation	
Name: A. Pierce		DATE: 30.7.88

For every Capital_Account_Record:
    1.1. If the Residual_Value is less than £250
        Then,
            Set Annual Depreciation to Residual_Value
            Set Residual_Value to zero
        Else,
            Set Annual_Depreciation to 10% of Residual_Value
            Reduce Residual_Value by 10%
    1.2. Debit Depreciation_Account with Annual_Depreciation

Example (a)

PROCESS ID:PPC 4.2.2	PROCESS NAME: Voltage Validy Check	
Name: S. Cripps		DATE: 2/2/88

REPEAT
    take a voltage reading
    IF it is over the critical limit **THEN**
        place it in the *invalid readings* block
    ELSE
        place it in the *valid readings* block
    END IF
UNTIL all the voltage readings have been dealt with

Example (b)

Figure 3.11 Examples of the use of structured English for transform specification.

Neither of the examples may be designated as a proposed standard, but they both include features that you may or may not regard as adding to the clarity of the presentation. In both examples we have used indentation. This is not mandatory but many people regard it as a useful habit to assume. In example (a), in addition, the constructs have been numbered. For items defined in the data dictionary, the convention has been adopted of capitalizing the first letter in each word of the item's name and linking the words with the underline character. In example (b), constructs are not numbered but reserved words (repeat, if, then, etc.) have been capitalized and emboldened. The names of stores have been italicized. Finally, note that each mini-spec header includes the process ID and process name. This provides the essential cross-referencing to the corresponding DFDs. In practice, other header information is required, e.g., date of preparation, analyst's name, and so on. Which of these features you use is entirely up to you. But do remember that although national and international standards may not exist, individual organizations might have their own standards. If you work for such a company you will be expected to conform to these standards.

Exercise 3.11 Express the following in structured English: 'Each works order refers to a quantity of each of several different sub-assemblies. Each works order that arrives is processed by accessing the parts list for the first sub-assembly and multiplying the number-off figure for each part, by the number of sub-assemblies required. For each part an allocation slip is prepared by inserting the allocated number (i.e., the product of number off and number of sub-assemblies required), part number, sub-assembly number and works order number. If the part number is for a bought-out part then the allocation slip is forwarded to the Material Control Department. Otherwise it is sent to the Data Entry Section. This is repeated for each sub-assembly on the works order.'

3.4.2 Data dictionaries

In order to round off the specification we need to record the composition of each flow and each file or store that has been shown on any of our levelled set of DFDs. This needs to be completed right down to the level of individual data items. For instance, let us return to the question of our purchase commitment system. We have constantly referred to the input to this system as being 'purchase order information'. We now have to be more specific and, once again, we will tackle this in a hierarchical fashion. For a start, there would have to be an entry for 'purchase order information' in the data dictionary. If we established that what we had been calling by this term really consisted of two different types of terminal transaction, 'purchase order' and 'payment advice', then we would require an entry for each of these too. Further, each data item occurring in either of these two would merit its own entry. It is clear that if we depended on natural language for compiling the entries we might have the same problems as if we used natural language for mini-specs, i.e. imprecision, ambiguity, and all the rest. We require some form of symbolism that will enable us to define flows and files precisely. Again DeMarco (1979) comes to the rescue with a notation for data dictionary definitions. We will examine it briefly.

Definition notation DeMarco (1979) proposes the use of a handful of simple symbols which seem to cover most circumstances that one is likely to encounter. Listed with their meanings they are as follows:

(a) = is equivalent to
(b) + and
(c) (A) optional
(d) {B} iterations of
(e) $\begin{bmatrix} C \\ D \end{bmatrix}$ either C or D (but not both)

Symbols (a) and (b) need no further explanation. Symbol (c) indicates that item A inside the brackets may or may not be present. As (d) stands it means that there can be anywhere between zero and an infinite number of items B present. However, it is possible to show limits if the analyst so desires. If there can be between two and five items B present, the symbolism is 2{B}5. The indication that there would be at least one present would be 1{B}. Symbol (e) is shown to represent the exclusive-OR situation. However, this may be changed by including C, D, and C + D within the square brackets, thus conveying that inclusive-OR applies. An example of the use of the symbols is given in Fig. 3.12.

Definition Part of Entry

Entry 1   payment = payment advice + 0{cheque}1
Entry 2   payment advice = date +   name of supplier
                              +   address of supplier
                              + $\begin{bmatrix} \text{cheque number} \\ \text{transfer details} \end{bmatrix}$
                              + {invoice no. + date
                                   + invoice amount + (narrative)}
                              +   payment total
Entry 3   cheque =   ?

Figure 3.12 Data dictionary definitions relating to an information flow.

The example is based on an organization that pays its suppliers by cheque or bank transfer. A payment advice is sent, accompanied by a cheque, when appropriate. The first entry is for the information flow, *payment*. However, this identifies the existence of two major components of the flow, *payment advice* and *cheque*, and these should be given entries of their own in the dictionary. Note that the presence of *payment advice* in the flow *payment* is mandatory, while *cheque* is optional. We show an entry for *payment advice* and this inevitably identifies further items that will require further entries.

The entry indicates that this component of the flow includes a date plus the name of the supplier and the address of the supplier. It also includes either the cheque number or the transfer details, and the details of from zero to an infinite number of invoices, and the payment total. Within the invoice detail there may or may not be narrative.

Exercise 3.12 There are two ways of showing that *there is at most one X present* using this notation. What are they?

Exercise 3.13 The entry for *cheque* in Fig. 3.12 has been left with a query sign. With reference to your own or someone else's cheque book, complete a definition for *cheque*.

Although we have confined our use of the dictionary notation to information flows, it is easy to see that it is just as applicable to defining files.

Exercise 3.14 A personnel file comprises between 3000 and 5000 records; each record includes *name, address, NI number* and, in some cases, *tax code*. Compile a data dictionary definition for the file.

Supplementary information You probably noted that Fig. 3.12 referred to the definition part of the entries and we are sure that the significance of the wording did not escape you. In fact, the dictionary entry is a highly suitable repository for a great deal of useful information about the flows and files. One feature of particular interest is the question of aliases. Frequently, the components of an information flow, particularly if they are documents, are known by different names by different parts of an organization. For instance, a simple document such as a goods received note (which records the delivery of material from outside the organization) may have several names: goods received note, GRN, goods inwards note, etc. Obviously, this can cause a certain amount of confusion unless account is taken of the aliases and so we need an effective and efficient way of incorporating them in the data dictionary.

One possibility would be to enter the full definition of the item under each of the aliases. This would be effective but inefficient, for the dictionary would contain repeated and, thus, redundant information. Apart from unnecessarily inflating the dictionary size the full enormity of this approach would be experienced when, for whatever reason, it became necessary to change the entry. Such changes would need to be replicated across all the aliases. Under pressure, it is only too likely that one or more entries might be overlooked. We would then have the very unsatisfactory situation of inconsistent definitions for the same flow. A better approach is the following. The analyst in consultation with the user determines which of the names is to be regarded as the official version, and the full definition is entered in the dictionary under this name. The entry should include a special section in which aliases are recorded. In addition, each alias should have its own brief entry which would consist only of its name and a cross-reference to the main entry.

Other information that might be included depends largely on personal taste. It would seem sensible that in the case of information flows, present and projected volumes could well be incorporated. For files or stores, the expected number of records and the method by which they are organized would seem to be sufficiently important to be included as a matter of course.

3.4.3 Summary

In Secs 3.4.1 and 3.4.2 we introduced some notations for transform specification and data dictionaries. These now complete the analyst's tool kit for recording the results of his or her investigations into the required functionality of the proposed software. Neither of the main notations that we discussed are the subject of strict convention, so that the analyst has a great deal of freedom in applying them. But we must emphasize the need to conform to any standard presentation that has been adopted by the analyst's organization. Freedom is a fine thing but many software disasters bear witness to its abuse.

3.5 SUMMARY OF REQUIREMENTS ANALYSIS

In this chapter we have tried to convey the philosophy of requirements analysis in so far as practice allows. In fact, practice will vary widely but philosophy should be immutable. We do not think we can do better at this stage than to list what we regard as being the basic tenets of the analyst's faith:

- adopt a careful top-down approach
- take nothing for granted but everything for the insight it provides
- validate each step as far as you are able
- adhere to standards if they exist; develop your own if they do not
- communicate your findings in a manner that is appropriate to your audience and finally
- do not try and do the designer's job, for your quest is for 'what', the designer's is for 'how'.

We are left finally with the question of the formal presentation or packaging of the results of the requirements analysis stage. This is the subject of the next chapter.

REFERENCE

DeMarco, T. (1979) *Structured Analysis and System Specification*, Prentice-Hall, Englewood Cliffs, New Jersey.

4

SPECIFICATION OF REQUIREMENTS

4.1 INTRODUCTION

As early as Sec. 2.3 we made a critical point about the specification of requirements and have mentioned it periodically ever since. That is, that the document has a dual role. On the one hand, it is the vehicle by which the user's agreement is secured. On the other, it is the most significant input to the design process. Accordingly, we took particular care in selecting notations so that, to the best of our ability, we would be in a position to create a document that would fufil this twin purpose. It is clear, therefore, that no matter what else it might contain it will incorporate the levelled set of dataflow diagrams, the mini-specs and the data dictionary so painstakingly compiled.

In Chapter 3, a further point was made. Arising from preliminary analysis of the user requirement document, Fig. 3.2, we noted that there were three independent flows of information that were not involved in requirements analysis but which, nevertheless, needed to be brought to the attention of the designers. These were non-functional requirements (arising from former design decisions), design objectives and true non-functional requirements. It was stated that it was common practice to formalize the communication of these items by incorporating them in the specification of requirements. We are thus beginning to build a structure for this document. However, other than the addition of the usual housekeeping items such as introduction, appendices, and so on, there is little more that can be said with any degree of certainty. Probably there are as many ideas on what the specification of requirements should contain as a whole, as there are users and designers. Consequently, we will content ourselves with examining a format that may be regarded as typical. This is shown as Fig. 4.1.

	Specification of Requirements
Section 1	Introduction 1.1 Functional summary 1.2 Assumptions
Section 2	Design objectives
Section 3	Functional requirements
Section 4	Non-functional requirements
Section 5	Quality assurance provisions 5.1 Software test procedures 5.2 Software validation procedures 5.3 Acceptance criteria
Section 6	Maintenance specification 6.1 Anticipated changes 6.2 Arrangements for error reporting

Figure 4.1 A format for the specification of requirements document.

4.2 DISCUSSION ON FORMAT

On the whole, Fig. 4.1 is self-explanatory and little further exposition is required. Section 1 is a conventional introduction to the document in that it summarizes the functions with which the software is concerned. Bearing in mind that the expected life of the software may be of the order of ten years or so, it will almost certainly have been necessary at some stage of requirements analysis to have made, with the user, some assumptions. These may have been in connection with projected message volumes, file sizes, the level of business activity or some other critical property. Accordingly, these assumptions need to be listed in the introductory material.

In Section 2, the design objectives emerging from the analysis of the user requirement document are recorded. These may be supplemented by other objectives that only came to light when serious discussions with the user began. This section is of critical importance to the designer, for it is from this that the criteria will be composed that will be used to drive selection throughout the design phase.

Section 3 will contain all the material pertinent to the required functionality of the software. Thus, it will include the levelled set of dataflow diagrams, the mini-specs for primitive transforms and the data dictionary.

The non-functional requirements of Section 4 will include both the former design decisions imposed by the user and the true constraints. Once again this section is of prime interest to the designer because of its power to reduce the amount of selection required.

In Section 5, an attempt is made to reassure the user with regard to the integrity of the final product. Quite apart from an explanation of the test procedures to which the software will be subjected, a description is given of the steps that will be taken to maintain consistency from stage to stage through the life cycle. A final sub-section lists the performance criteria that will need to be met before the system is regarded as acceptable by the user. For instance, if the new software involves querying a database, one acceptance criterion might be that 99 per cent of transactions should trigger a response in 5 seconds or less.

Finally, Section 6 will outline any expected changes to the operating environment and the means of coping with these changes. And in anticipation of the errors that inevitably will appear once the software is in service, the procedures for reporting them and the prospective maintenance arrangements are detailed.

SUMMARY AND FURTHER READING I

5.1 SUMMARY OF CHAPTERS 1–4

We began this book by introducing the idea of the software life cycle and the staged approach to the development of new software. After a brief review of each stage we concentrated on requirements analysis and its precedent and subsequent documentation, the user requirement document and the specification of requirements. To assist in the preparation of the latter, a view based on information flow was adopted, the corresponding dataflow diagram notation was described and its use demonstrated. It was then shown how the illustration of required functionality could be completed with an appropriate transform specification technique, structured English, and a data dictionary.

We concluded the first part of the book by reviewing the nature and role of the specification of requirements and examining one of the many structures that such a document might possess.

5.2 FURTHER READING

Good introductions to dataflow diagrams, transform specification and data dictionaries are provided in each of the following:

T. DeMarco, *Structured Analysis and System Specification*, Prentice-Hall, Englewood Cliffs, New Jersey, 1979.

C. Gane and T. Sarson, *Structured Systems Analysis: Tools and Techniques*, Prentice-Hall, Englewoods Cliffs, New Jersey, 1979.

The former, of course, has been quoted liberally in the forgoing text. If one can forgive his rather jokey and light-hearted treatment of such a serious subject then it is highly recommended. Gane and Sarson cover much the same ground although their DFD symbolism differs slightly from that of DeMarco. Both books may be criticized for an almost total concentration on commercial data processing. It is hoped, however, that the chapters you have just read have made clear that the dataflow view is applicable over a much wider class of computer applications.

Some discussion of structured analysis and specification is normally to be found in modern texts on software engineering. Usually the treatment is relatively cursory for such books are devoted to the life cycle as a whole, and much else besides. Typical of books of this type is:

R. S. Pressman, *Software Engineering: a Practitioner's Approach*, 2nd edn, McGraw-Hill London, 1987.

There seems to be a minor industry developing in the field of handbooks devoted to analysis, specification and design, in which the structured techniques receive due mention. A recent book of this type which, despite the title, is a serious contribution to the literature is:

D. Connor, *Information System Specification and Design Road Map*, Prentice-Hall, Englewood Cliffs, New Jersey, 1985.

These texts are valuable in providing comparisons between different methodologies but in order to obtain a useful working knowledge of any particular techniques it is usually necessary to refer to the primary sources.

SOFTWARE DESIGN

6.1 REVIEW OF THE SOFTWARE LIFE CYCLE

Earlier in this book we had cause to introduce a concept known as the Software Life Cycle. We studied the life cycle via a graphical model which is reproduced as Fig. 6.1. As modelled, the cycle is a consecutive sequence of phases, each phase being initiated and terminated by the introduction or production of documents. It is worth repeating an earlier caution. As the model is a graphical representation of a physical process, not everyone will adopt the same view, so that variations on the model abound. But this need not cause any confusion as the basic activities will always be the same. At the time of our first meeting with the concept we were almost entirely concerned with the first stage, requirements analysis, and the documents that served to delimit its scope, i.e., the user requirement document and the specification of requirements. So that, except for a brief introduction, the other stages received little attention. We must now focus our attention on to the second stage, design, and the question that we did our best to avoid during requirements analysis, namely, how software functionality is to be achieved.

6.2 INPUTS TO THE DESIGN STAGE

The major formal input to the design stage is the specification of requirements. A brief recapitulation of the contents of this document indicates that it contains, among others, sections on functional requirements, non-functional requirements or constraints, and design objectives. The functional requirements provide the designer with the main raw material on which he or she is to work. The constraints have the effect of removing

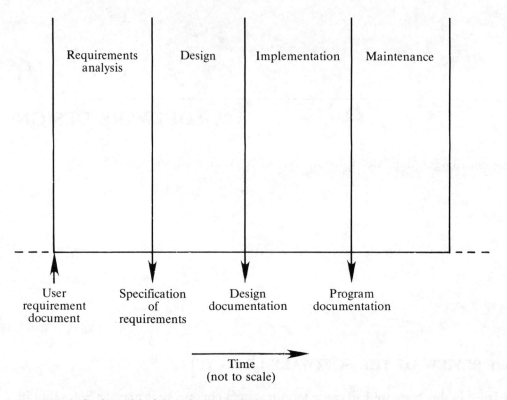

Figure 6.1 A simple model of the software life cycle.

certain categories of design from the design process, and the design objectives indicate to the designer the features or properties of the software that are valued most highly by the user. Although it is convenient to regard the specification of requirements as the last word in user-desired functionality, life is rarely quite that simple. The specification can never be regarded as cast in bronze for the designer will inevitably discern ambiguities or circumstances that lack clarity so that a temporary return to the requirements stage and a subsequent modification to the specification will be called for.

In addition to the formal inputs to design there will be informal ones as well. This is particularly true of design objectives for these are rarely conveyed explicitly and in full, from the user to the designer. In this context, the most significant input is probably the designer's own experience and this matter is considered further in a later section.

6.3 OUTPUTS FROM THE DESIGN STAGE

In Fig. 6.1 we show the outputs under the comprehensive heading of design documentation. However, this may consist of a number of separate documents each with a separate and distinct purpose. In our original treatment of the life cycle we highlighted the design document as being the main vehicle for conveying the chosen design to the programmers who will convert it into operational computer programs. Other outputs might include a systems manual which is intended as a guide to those responsible for maintaining the system once it is in operation, and a user manual which we identified as the key reference for the people who will actually use the system. The provision of a user guide or tutorial as a training aid was also mentioned as a possibility. In this chapter we are mainly concerned with the design document and its provision. Consequently, our discussion will mainly centre on design strategy and appropriate notations to communicate with programmers. The other documents are very user- and application-dependent so that we will do no more than indicate guidelines for their preparation.

6.4 ASPIRATIONS OF THE SYSTEMS DESIGNER

A genius once said that being a genius amounted to one per cent inspiration and ninety-nine per cent perspiration, and give or take a few per cent, the same comment applies to systems design. With the understanding that we now have of the design process it is conceivable that anyone with the basic computing skills who is diligent, honest and generally sober could design a good system. With the addition of some experience and the odd flash of inspiration, very good designs are likely.

The reason why a broad class of humans could design good, if not very good systems is exactly the same as the reason why a large number of people could be good burglars. There are in existence a number of well developed procedures that have been shown to give good results. Although in the world of software design, if not burglary, we talk of design strategy. The application of a good design strategy enables a good design to be sketched out in a straightforward manner, albeit with some effort. Converting it to a very good design requires the aforementioned experience and inspiration.

It will be noted that we have spoken of the quality of designs in very general terms, i.e., good and very good. You may well enquire at this point as to how one finds the best design. The answer is that you cannot or, at least, the probability of doing so is so small that it can be ignored for all practical purposes. The reason for this will soon become apparent.

7

SELECTION

7.1 PROBLEM-SOLVING AND DECISION-MAKING

It is helpful at this stage to introduce the ideas of problem solving, a structure for which was first described by Dewey (1910). The stages identified by John Dewey were: What is the problem? What are the alternatives? Which alternative is best? You should now be in a position to identify a resemblance between Dewey's three stages and the software life cycle.

Enough has been said about the life cycle earlier for us to spot a distinct resemblance between the first stage of problem definition and our requirements analysis phase. In fact many organizations use the term 'problem' or 'project definition' rather than 'requirements analysis'. The final two stages may similarly be identified as being equivalent to the phase that we refer to as 'design'.

A more recent, but very relevant structure has been supplied in the context of decision-making (Simon, 1960). Professor Simon labels the stages of decision-making as follows: Intelligence activity, Design activity and Choice activity.

The term 'Intelligence' is used here in the military sense, i.e., searching the environment for conditions requiring a decision to be made. 'Design' is concerned with inventing and developing possible courses of action. The activity of selecting a particular course of action from those available is known as 'Choice'. In this case our requirements analysis corresponds to the intelligence activity. Although the software designer does not need to search too hard for circumstances requiring a decision to be made, they will normally be found lying on his or her desk labelled 'Specification of requirements'.

However Simon's use of the term 'Design' differs from ours. Whereas Simon uses the word to describe the generation of possible solutions, we use it in the sense that selection is included also.

There seems to be some justification for believing that problem-solving, decision-making and software analysis and design share a common framework. And it is not stretching the point too far to claim that the first two are, in effect, exactly the same thing while the last is just a particular instance of this phenomenon. Consequently, we shall persist in regarding software design as a problem-solving activity and treating it as such. This means that we must devote some attention to the questions of generating possible solutions (i.e., designs), and the selection of one from this number.

7.2 SIZE OF SELECTION

Let us start with a very simple design problem. As one of the parents of a nuclear family you decide to take your spouse and your two and a half children to Scarborough for the day. Your design problem is to establish the best way of making the journey. You establish the alternatives as being: British Rail, National Bus or private car.

In order to make your choice you need something else. You cannot possibly decide which is the best unless there is some property possessed by the three alternatives which is important to you and which you wish to see maximized or minimized. Hence, if you wish to minimize the cost of the outing, say, the decision is soon made, given some understanding of the fare structures of British Rail and National, and a realistic appraisal of the fuel consumption of your car. Such a property, in this case the direct costs of the journey, is known as the design criterion or design objective. Similarly, you might take journey time as the design criterion and once again the study of timetables and knowledge of your car's capabilities would enable a ready choice to be made. In passing, we should note that if both costs and journey time are important then the choice might be more difficult. But the latter point is for future development. For the moment we must concentrate on size of selection.

7.2.1 Combinatorial explosion

In the foregoing example the design problem was trivial, for the selection had to be made from three alternatives, each one of which was easily evaluated. But now recall that sometime in the past we asked you to determine the number of possible designs that existed if you were faced with the problem of adding three numbers. We concluded that four designs were possible and in Fig. 7.1 we show them by inventing and using a device that we might call an adding tree.

As is usual in computing, the trees are upside down with the root pointing to the stars, but the representation is plain. The leaves of the trees represent the original numbers, symbolized as *A, B* and *C.* The branches represent the flow of numbers and sub-totals up the tree, terminating with the total at the root. Where branches meet we have what we may call a *node* and at each of these a simple addition takes place.

It is not too difficult to calculate the number of designs that are possible for adding five numbers. In fact, there are 236 possible designs and a handful of the corresponding adding trees are illustrated in Fig. 7.2.

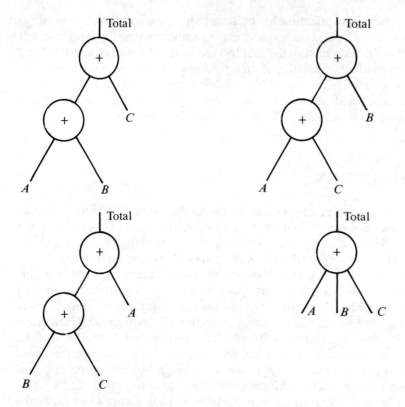

Figure 7.1 Four designs for adding three numbers.

This is a considerable increase over the four possible designs for adding three numbers and is an example of what is sometimes known as the combinatorial explosion. In other words, when faced with considering different ways of combining a number of elements, you rapidly arrive at a large number of alternatives as the number of elements increases. You may recall from an earlier chapter that the deceptively simple problem of adding fifty numbers generated 6.85×10^{81} designs — a conversation-stopper if we ever met one.

The design of a substantial piece of software poses a similar problem: a very large number of alternatives all of which, in theory, need to be examined and assessed if the best design is to be selected. We say, in theory, because if we calculate how long it takes to assess each design, we will immediately see that a comeprehensive assessment of all designs is not possible. If, using electronic means, say, it takes one-millionth of a second to examine and assess each of the possible adding trees for fifty numbers, how long would it take to select (i.e., design) the optimum tree?

This particular design problem would take 2.17×10^{66} centuries to complete thus indicating that on the face of it and except for trivial cases, design is impossible. Nevertheless all over the world and everyday, people are designing systems, and some of them are quite good. So we must now consider how so many intelligent people knowingly attempt the impossible, often to good effect.

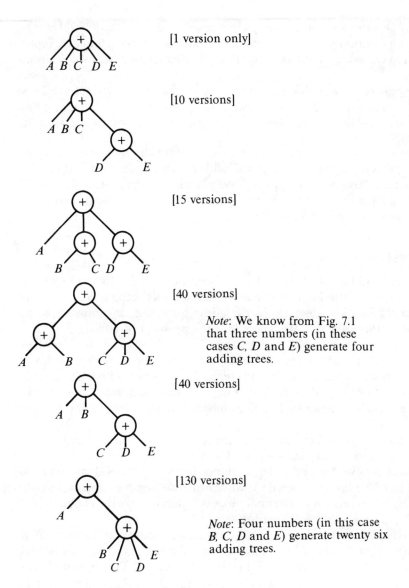

[1 version only]

[10 versions]

[15 versions]

[40 versions]

Note: We know from Fig. 7.1 that three numbers (in these cases *C*, *D* and *E*) generate four adding trees.

[40 versions]

[130 versions]

Note: Four numbers (in this case *B, C, D* and *E*) generate twenty six adding trees.

Figure 7.2 Some adding trees for five numbers.

7.2.2 Constraints

Design, in general, is helped considerably if as many alternatives as possible may be struck out before the attempt at selection begins. Constraints do exactly this. We first met constraints in the guise of non-functional requirements when examining the requirements analysis phase of the Software Life Cycle. We found that they are often stated explicitly in the user requirement document and frequently relate to hardware, software, time or money. Hence, a statement to the effect that new software is to be implemented on an Olivetti M24 successfully eliminates all designs that could not be implemented thereon. Similarly, a non-functional requirement that standard input/ output software is to be used, cuts out all those designs involving purpose-built input/ output software.

Time and money also constrain design. If it is essential that the software is available for operational use by a certain date, then all designs that are so complex that they could not meet the deadline must be rejected. Similarly, designs that will cost in excess of the user's budget to implement must go.

Although the application of constraints can severely limit the number of choices available to the designer, the size of selection will still seem unmanageable. After all a very large number, less a large number, is still a very large number. So a designer still needs some help in tackling the selection problem. This help comes in the form of what are termed design *heuristics* or, if you prefer, rules-of-thumb.

7.2.3 Design heuristics

Let us turn again to the problem of adding fifty numbers and its 6.85×10^{81} adding trees. Just suppose that it is possible to identify five of the numbers as being related in some way so that they could be close together in the adding tree, e.g., they are all octal, perhaps, whereas the others are not. We know that the prospect of adding these five numbers will give rise to 236 possible adding trees. The evaluation of the 236 alternatives is perfectly feasible and the optimal adding sub-tree for these five numbers could be selected. We would then be able to replace the five numbers with a single node representing the optimal adding sub-tree. So that we have now achieved a reduction in the numbers to be added from 50 to 46, i.e., 45 numbers and a sub-total from the sub-tree.

The process could be repeated taking five numbers at a time and replacing them, similarly, with a single satisfactory sub-tree or design.

The process would involve thirteen cycles, each one involving the evaluation of 236 designs, except the last. The last cycle would involve only two numbers and this would permit only one design. Consequently, the total process would involve the evaluation of 12×236, i.e., 2832 separate designs (Emery, 1969).

Even with this reduction in the number of separate designs, there is still a lot to do. If it takes a quarter of an hour to examine and assess each alternative, how long would it take to design the optimal adding tree using the above procedure? Design would now take 708 hours. Or, assuming that one designer is working on the problem, just under 18 working man-weeks. So that design is no longer impossible but merely tedious and formidable.

The above is an example of a design heuristic, a rule-of-thumb used by the designer to reduce drastically the size of selection until it becomes a manageable problem. The source of such design heuristics may be experience or the native cunning of the designer, or it may be part of the folklore of the profession.

The similarity with folklore does not stop there. You are, no doubt, familiar with a number of folkloric expressions of the 'red sky at night, shepherds' delight' type. On hearing this from the lips of some weather-beaten sage, one can almost hear the quotation marks. And so it is with designers. The expert at designing adding trees for fifty numbers, when holding forth in the local drinking establishment, might well say:

Take five numbers that for some reason should be close together on the tree, replace them with a single node representing the optimal sub-tree, and repeat until one tree remains.

Spoken with almost-audible quotation marks such a statement may take on the authority of holy writ, and therein lies a danger. The danger is that a particular heuristic may have been regarded so favourably by practitioners that it is taken to be a fundamental truth. The trouble is that times change and, particularly in computing, so does technology. So that a design heuristic that has been used successfully for some time may rapidly become obsolete and untrustworthy.

Despite these difficulties, design could not take place at all without heuristics. You will find soon that design strategy usually makes use of them, and they also play an important part in 'polishing' or refining a first design acquired by other techniques. Thus part of a designer's skill lies in his or her ability, not only to apply heuristics, but also to choose them with care.

Exercise 7.1 What do you regard as the basic weakness of the design heuristic as used above?

7.3 DESIGN CRITERIA

We commenced Sec. 7.2 with a simple problem, designing the transportation arrangements for a family day-out to the seaside. We noted that with three alternatives and a single criterion, direct costs or journey time, the problem is trivial. But we also stated that if both criteria are important then the design problem becomes rather more difficult. To take this matter a little further, let us suppose that the parent decision-maker, from the information available about fare structures, timetables and so on, has assembled the table shown as Fig. 7.3.

Mode of transport	Direct costs	Journey time
P	£10.20	55 mins
Q	£ 7.85	80 mins
R	£ 5.60	105 mins

Figure 7.3 Journey information for a day at Scarborough.

The three modes of transport are called *P, Q* and *R* to disguise our own prejudices. For each mode, estimates of direct costs and journey time are entered. It is clear that if direct cost is the sole criterion then *R* is favourite; if journey time is of lone importance then *P* wins, hands down. Try and imagine yourself in the position of the parent decision-maker. On the basis of the information in Fig. 7.3, what would *your* choice be? (Just for once we are not concerned with your actual answer but only with how you arrived at it.)

If you arrived at a decision, and whether your answer was *P, Q* or *R*, you almost certainly got there by using the process of *trading off*, although you may not have been aware that you were so doing.

You probably posed yourself questions such as: 'is it worth incurring extra costs of £2.35 in order to save 25 minutes on the journey?' and from the answers that you gave yourself, you arrived at your conclusion.

You may also have thought that it was a daft question for, in practice, you would need to take other properties or attributes into account, e.g., comfort, convenience and if Aunt Gloria insists on coming (as she usually does), the scenic beauty of the route, perhaps. You may have noted at the same time that these three attributes of the transport mode are intangible, so that trading them off against direct costs is a non-starter anyway.

You may also have toyed with ideas of uncertainty, bearing in mind that engineering works, traffic jams, staff shortages and breakdowns could completely invalidate the stated journey times. These complaints are quite reasonable but, nevertheless, people *do* take decisions like the one we have been discussing here, all the time. Largely, they will use a combination of trading off and intuition. But it should be noted that selection can be formalized to take all the factors mentioned above into account, by developing what is known as a multi-attribute utility function. However, these are deep waters and we had better turn back before we all sink.

7.3.1 Pressures and criteria

So far, we have not considered *why* the family decision-maker in the previous section lighted upon direct costs and journey time as the exclusive design criteria. If we think about this carefully we realize that this is due to pressures being brought to bear on the decision-maker. We do not exclude such pressures being self-generated but it is simpler to regard them as arising from outside. We are then able to represent the situation neatly and graphically by a sketch as in Fig. 7.4.

We see now the origins of the design criteria. The thrifty spouse is insisting on low costs; impatient children are demanding a short journey time. No doubt Aunt Gloria (who likes nothing better than dozing in National Park car parks and is filthy rich the bargain), if she existed, would also be exerting a pressure that would be well-nigh irresistible. So that the decision will be taken in an attempt to resolve these pressures to the satisfaction of all. Or at least, so that not too much dissatisfaction is experienced by anybody. We can note also that the trading off process will be conditioned by the relative weights that the decision-maker places on the competing pressures.

The idea of associating weights with pressures is fundamental to the activities of the software designer, to whom we must now return.

7.3.2 Pressures and software design

When studying earlier material concerning the software life cycle you were asked to complete an exercise (Exercise 2.2) asking for your views on the attributes or properties to be taken into account when comparing software designs. In the solution to the exercise it was suggested that they were many and various but that a list of the most important ones would include:

Minimize
costs

Minimize
Journey time

Figure 7.4 Pressures on family decision-maker,

Economy, Reliability, Maintainability, Robustness, Integrity, Security

The definitions for the first three are reasonably obvious. But what do you understand by *robustness, integrity* and *security*? You will recall from the exercise solution that by robustness we mean the capability of a system to handle variations in volumes of trans-actions. Integrity and security are more difficult to define with any authority as very often they are used interchangeably. The authors' preference is to use the term 'integrity' to describe resistance to *accidental* corruption or destruction of programs and data. Whereas 'security' applies to a system's resistance to *deliberate* damage.

The point that we are coming to is that we are now examining another pressure situation, one that is illustrated in Fig. 7.5.

The pressures are shown as originating with the user as a single entity. In practice, of course, different individuals and departments within the user organization will have different vested interests in the software performance and the pressures that they exert will differ accordingly. But the designer is in exactly the same position as the harassed parent in the previous section, needing to resolve the design problem in such a way that the user's satisfaction is maximized.

The designer really needs some composite measure that could be derived for every competing design, which reflects as closely as possible the user's comparative rating of the attributes for importance and makes due allowance for uncertainty. What the designer really needs, therefore, is a multi-attribute utility function. But we have shied away from this once and we shall do so again. The excuse for being so chicken is that such functions are incredibly difficult to derive in the software design context, so that no designer ever attempts to do so.

However, in very limited circumstances (which we shall explain later) a designer *may* feel obliged to introduce some objectivity into his or her selection mechanism. This will usually involve a development of the trading off process that we have already encountered and requires the application of what is known as the *value function*. In the simplest terms this means forming a weighted average of individual attributes. For instance, we might represent the value of a software design $V(S)$, as follows:

$$\{c1 \times \text{\textit{value of attribute 1}}\} + \{c2 \times \text{\textit{value of attribute 2}}\} + \{c3 \times \text{\textit{value of attribute 3}}\} + \ldots + \{cn \times \text{\textit{value of attribute n}}\} \tag{1}$$

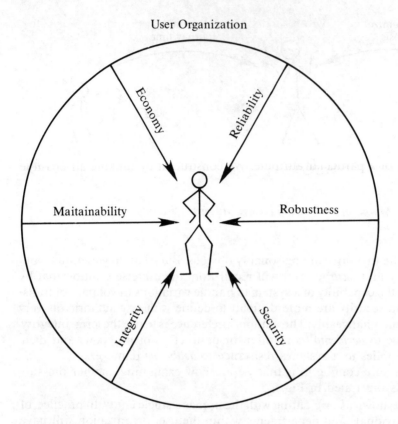

Figure 7.5 Pressures on a software designer.

where $c1, c2, c3, \ldots, cn$ are weighting factors.

It is often convenient to represent both the value of any one attribute and the value of the combination of attributes over a standard range, say from 0 to 100. In these circumstances, the condition $(c1 + c2 + c3 + \ldots + cn = 1)$ is imposed (Chapman, 1980).

In order to demonstrate the use of the value function let us assume that a designer is due to make a final choice from three candidates designs. We will assume also that the pressures on the designer are limited to three: economy, reliability and robustness. The data relative to the three designs is assembled in Fig. 7.6.

Design	Economy (£'000 per year)	Reliability (per cent availability)	Robustness (per cent tolerance)
X	20	95	17.5
Y	27.5	96	20
Z	32	99	10

Figure 7.6 Data for three software designs.

The diagram shows for each of the designs, X, Y and Z, the estimated attribute values for each design criterion. You will note that we represent economy by the operating costs of the system in thousands of pounds per year. The measure of reliability is percentage availablity, i.e., the proportion of time that the software is expected to be functioning correctly. Robustness is represented by the percentage tolerances on the volume that the system is being designed to handle. Our first move must now be to construct a value function for each attribute.

Value function — single attribute A value function merely expresses the desirability of different 'quantities' of a particular attribute. We construct it by ranking all possible values for the attribute in order of desirability, assigning 0 to the least desirable, 100 to the most desirable and appropriate values in the range 0 to 100 to the others. We might thus arrive at value functions for the three criteria of interest to us, as in Fig. 7.7.

The functions should represent, as far as can possibly be determined, the values of the attributes to the user. Note that the functions are not necessarily linear although we have shown two of them as being so. Note also that we show the *worst* result at the left-hand side of the horizontal axis and the *best* result at the right. This means that for economy, for which low results are preferred, the scale *decreases* from left to right. For the other two, it *increases* from left to right. We now have to combine the value information available to us into one expression to represent the value of each design as a whole.

Value function — multi-attribute We can evaluate each of the three competing designs in terms of economy, reliability and robustness by using a version of expression (1) p. 49:

$$V(S) = \{c1 \times \textit{value of economy}\} + \{c2 \times \textit{value of reliability}\} + \{c3 \times \textit{value of robustness}\} \tag{2}$$

All that remains is to assign values to the three weighting factors $c1$, $c2$ and $c3$ and these evaluations should reflect the relative severity of the corresponding pressures on the designer.

Exercise 7.2 The designer estimates that the three constants should be assigned values as follows: $c1 = 0.2$, $c2 = 0.5$, $c3 = 0.3$. Which design would you expect to be selected?

Exercise 7.3 Faced with the same design problem as in exercise 7.2, another designer concludes that the user regards the economy criterion and the robustness criterion as being equally important, while reliability is regarded as only half as important as either. Would the new designer make the same choice?

Summary There is a certain amount of caution to be observed if serious use is to be made of the multi-attribute value function. First, a theoretical condition, known as *preferential independence* must be met. This condition is only satisfied if preferences which

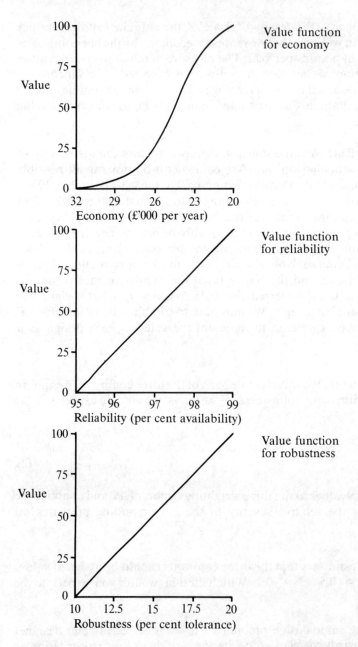

Figure 7.7 Sample value functions for economy, reliability and robustness.

hold between any pair of attributes are independent of the values of any other attributes. For instance, if a design with estimated operating costs of £25 000 per year and 97 per cent availability is preferred to a design with operating costs of £30 000 per year and 99 per cent availability, when both have a volume tolerance of 20 per cent, then the condition requires that the same preference should apply if the volume tolerance of both were to change to 15 per cent. It is not too difficult to imagine circumstances where the condition is violated. And maybe our example is a case in point. Perhaps in the eyes of many users, if volume tolerance is reduced as above, then availability becomes more significant and the preference might be reversed.

A second difficulty lies in the choice of weighting factors. We saw in Exercise 7.3 how a casual change in the factors threw up a new best design. A mere reaction to conflicting pressures on the part of the designer may not be an adequate mechanism for valuing the factors. It may be necessary to adopt more formal methods for deriving them. These involve asking hypothetical questions of the user personnel and are very time-consuming, particularly if a large number of criteria are involved, which is usually the case. An excellent description of the techniques is given in Chapman (1980).

A final difficulty which tends to dwarf all others is that many important design criteria are not easily quantifiable. An example is maintainability, a prior measure for which is difficult to conceive, so that any numerically based choice regime is equally difficult to implement.

For these reasons, it is unlikely that a designer will use value functions for the bulk of the selection task. It is much more likely that he or she will use simple trade off techniques based on what is known of user preferences, supported by intuition, as a rough sieve to eliminate the most unlikely designs. More sophisticated value techniques will only be brought to bear once the number of competing designs has been reduced to a reasonably small number.

7.4 SUMMARY OF SELECTION

We commenced this chapter by drawing an analogy between problem-solving and decision-making on the one hand, and software design on the other. We then continued to discuss design on the basis that it is a specialized branch of problem-solving. This enabled us to concentrate on the fundamental design activity which is that of making a choice. However, we were able to identify two major difficulties facing the designer of software.

First of all, there is *size of selection*. One design must be chosen for implementation, but this may be one of, perhaps, many million candidates, and the individual assessment of each one is physically impossible. We noted how non-functional requirements perform a valuable role as constraints, i.e., they eliminate many possible designs from consideration. But ultimately, the designer needs to fall back on the use of design heuristics or rules-of-thumb, in order to reduce the selection problem from the horrific to the feasible. However, apparently useful heuristics can rapidly become obsolete, so that care in their selection is advised.

The second major difficulty lies with the criteria by which designs are to be measured and compared. We saw that *design criteria* or *objectives* result from various pressures on the designer to *optimize* certain attributes of the software. An examination of formal approaches to evaluating designs indicated that they had severe drawbacks and, if used, it would be only when the selection of possible designs had been reduced to a handful or so. We concluded that the main evaluation tools used by the designer are simple trade off techniques and the designer's own judgement and intuition. But even so, some feeling for the relative weights to be assigned to the different design criteria is of prime importance. So far we have been rather theoretical. We now need to introduce some techniques that will actually allow us to *design* software. This will make a refreshing change from moaning about how difficult it all is.

REFERENCES

Chapman, M (1980) *Decision Analysis*, Civil Service Handbook No. 21, HMSO, London.
Dewey, J. (1910) *How We Think*, D. C. Heath & Co., New York.
Emery, J. C. (1969) *Organisational Planning and Control Systems*, Macmillan, London.
Simon, H. A. (1960) *The New Science of Management Decision*, Harper & Row, London.

INITIAL DESIGN

8.1 INTRODUCTION

A very popular word in computing is *methodology*, and it is methodology that we shall discuss now. It would be nice to provide a neat definition of the word, but it must be confessed that the writers do not know of one. It should be sufficient to say that we are interested in a systematic approach that will allow us to proceed from point A (the receipt of the specification of requirements) to point B (the issue of design documentation). Of course, there are many such approaches. We shall concentrate on one.

The one that we have chosen is popular and has an extra advantage for those who employ the dataflow view of life. This, you will recall from earlier chapters, includes us. The designs that result from the approach have an important feature in that they tend to be highly maintainable but this is at the expense of program efficiency. In terms of the previous chapter, the procedures that we shall use assume that the user places a relatively high weighting on maintainability compared with economy. As this approach also makes the control of design, programming and program testing rather easier, many users seem happy, or as happy as users ever are, with this state of affairs.

The approach that we will follow is based on a technique known as *structured design* (Yourdon and Constantine, 1979). A similar approach, known as *composite design*, is also relevant (Myers, 1975). It consists of three distinct activities which we can regard as taking place in sequence and which are illustrated in Fig. 8.1.

The diagram provides a close-up view of the design phase as it occurs in the Software Life Cycle, flanked by requirements analysis and implementation. Several documents are produced.

The name of the document which triggers off the design activities at point A on the horizontal axis is the prime output of the requirements analysis phase, the *specification of requirements*.

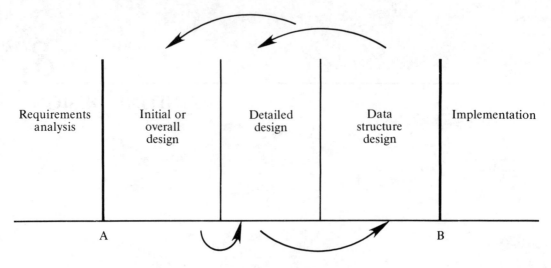

Figure 8.1 The activities of software design.

The *design document* which is the main means of communicating with programmers will definitely be produced at point B. The *systems manual*, the *user manual* and the *user guide* may be produced as well at this point.

This documentation, as a whole, is frequently referred to, rather confusingly, as the *design documentation*.

From Fig. 8.1 it can be seen that the first activity is known as *initial* or *overall design*. It is concerned with the first attempts to establish the overall 'shape' of the software by dividing it into basic blocks and determining the ways in which they should interface with each other. The second activity, *detailed design*, involves taking each basic block and defining the processing that should take place therein. The final activity, which is concerned with choosing the data structures that will be involved in the processing, is called *data structure design*.

Although we have shown the three activities as taking place in sequence, this is a practical oversimplification. For, much as progress through the main Software Life Cycle is iterative, so is progress through the design phase. In fact, so closely meshed are detailed design and data structure design technically, that we can almost regard them as parallel operations. And, of course, problems with these two activities may call for a return visit to initial design. An attempt has been made to represent these interconnections by means of arrows on the diagram.

We now need to look in some detail at the three activities thus identified. The remainder of this chapter will be concerned with *initial design*. Chapters 9 and 10 will deal with *detailed design* and *data structure design* respectively.

8.2 MODULARITY

We have already said that it has been accepted for some time that software is best designed and implemented as a set of small, more easily handled pieces. These pieces are the basic blocks referred to in the previous section and are termed *modules*.

Formally, a module is "a lexically contiguous sequence of program statements, bounded by boundary elements and having an aggregate identifier" (Yourdon and Constantine, 1979). By, *lexically contiguous* we merely mean that, *as written*, the program statements are adjacent. Note that because of such things as optimizing compilers and virtual memory, the lexical sequence *may* differ from the order in which the translated statements appear in memory. And because of control transfers, lexical order will frequently differ from execution order. By *boundary elements* we mean, for example, the statements *begin* and *end* which delimit a Pascal program. *Aggregate identifier* means only that a module has a name by which it may be referenced as a complete entity.

A module may be called or invoked by other modules. If a module is invoked it will usually, but not always, be supplied with input by the invoker, i.e., the calling module. It will then carry out its designed function and return the results to the invoker, if so required.

The term 'module' embraces sub-routines in the broadest sense and specific programming language variants, such as

Fortran — function
Cobol — sub-program, section or paragraph
PL/1 — procedure

We could regard a Pascal *function* as being equivalent. However, the function is too restrictive to meet many of the demands that we shall make. As we shall see, we will often require a module to return several results, or to provide a result that is an array or a record. Thus, a Pascal *procedure* more closely meets the definition.

But from this point on we must try and forget about these specific language variants, for design loses much of its utility if it becomes too closely tied to an implementation language. We shall thus use the term *module* and none other. If you encounter the words *function* or *procedure* from now on, you will know that they are being used in the general sense and should not be given the more limited Pascal interpretation, or for that matter, any interpretation limited by a particular language.

Initial design is concerned with modelling the software that is to be built as a set of inter-related modules, by a process that is known as *partitioning*. The output of this sub-phase is, accordingly, a graphical representation of the model, known as a *structure chart*. The structure chart is concerned, not only with the identification of the modules, but also with the specification of the interfaces between them.

8.3 STRUCTURE CHARTS

So once again, we use a simple picture to represent the initial design, once it has been chosen. An example of such a chart, incorporating the most important symbols, is shown as Fig. 8.2.

The figure shows the results of partitioning as a tree-like structure. The five rectangles represent five separate modules, each one with a distinctive, and one hopes,

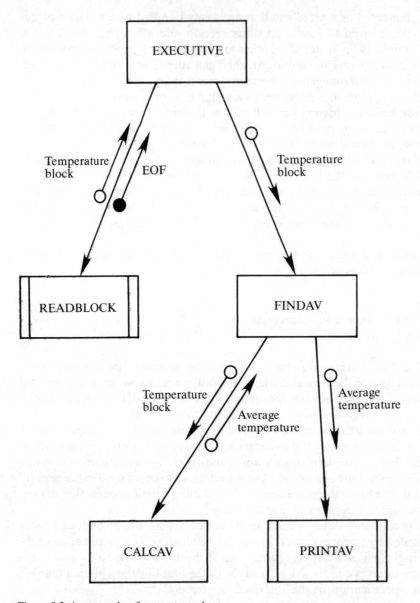

Figure 8.2 An example of a structure chart.

indicative name or identifier. In passing, it is common practice to name the top level module in such a way that it represents the program as a whole. So we would be quite justified in re-labelling Fig. 8.2 as the structure chart for the program EXECUTIVE. Two of the modules are drawn slightly differently from the other three in that the rectangle is striped, i.e., it has a vertical bar at each end. The significance of the stripes is that the module is pre-defined. In other words, it is a piece of software that is already in existence and not a new creation of the designers. This symbolism is usually employed if a suitable module already exists in an applications library or is part of the operating software.

In this case the two modules READBLOCK and PRINTAV have identifiers which, if truly indicative, seem to indicate that they are concerned with input and output, respectively. It is likely, therefore, that the use of standard operating software is being called for.

The next item to note is that some of the modules are connected by large downward-pointing arrows. These arrows are a fundamental device for indicating which modules are available for calling by others. Thus, READBLOCK and FINDAV may be called by EXECUTIVE, but not by any other. Similarly, CALCAV and PRINTAV are invokable by FINDAV only. No other calls are possible. We shall find it convenient on occasion to use some extra terminology in this context. When discussing a pair of modules, one of which can call the other, we may refer to the calling module as the *superordinate* and the called module as the *subordinate*. Thus, FINDAV is a subordinate of EXECUTIVE but also the superordinate of CALCAV.

The sole remaining feature to be explained is the presence of the small arrows lying parallel to the large arrows representing call availability. These represent the exchange of information between two modules that is implicit in a call, such items of information being known generally as *parameters*. Naturally, the heads of the arrows indicate the directions of information flow. The items of information may be single bits or characters, individual data items, or almost any data structure that you care to name. For instance, Fig. 8.2 shows that when FINDAV calls CALCAV it supplies it with the parameter *temperature block*, which is probably an array, and returns the result *average temperature*, which would be a single data item.

You will have noted that the parameter symbols are of two types. All but one of those in Fig. 8.2 are shown with a small circle at the blunt end of the arrow. This represents a parameter type known as a *data couple*. Such a parameter consists of information, the processing of which is essential to the functionality of the software. Both *temperature block* and *average temperature* are of this type. The remaining parameter sports a blob at the base of its arrow and is known as a *flag*. This represents a flow of control information. In other words it conveys a state of affairs rather than makes any positive contribution to functionality. Or, if you wish, it communicates information about the real data (Page-Jones, 1980). Thus, EOF is intended to indicate that if READBLOCK when attempting to do its duty finds that all the temperature blocks have been read and that the end of the file has been reached, then it is required to report the fact to its superordinate. EXECUTIVE.

Exercise 8.1 Write down in your own words what you believe the program EXECUTIVE is intended to achieve and what the role of each module is designed to be.

It is equally important for us to appreciate the things that the structure chart does *not* tell us. It does not tell us anything much about the structure of the modules. We know that FINDAV is able to call both CALCAV and PRINTAV and, consequently will, when implemented, include at least one call statement for each. However, there may be more than one such statement in each case. Both types of call statement may occur within a normal straightforward statement sequence. Equally, one or both of them may occur in a selection construct or within a loop, nested or otherwise. Finally, we do not know how often they will be called or even if, on a particular run, they will be called at all. In summary, therefore, the structure chart conveys the fact that certain modules are available to be called by others, and specifies the interface for each possible case. The omission of the other factors is not accidental but deliberate policy.

8.4 EVALUATION OF PARTITIONING

Obviously, there are many ways of partitioning a particular system into an initial design. Some initial designs are better than others. We need, therefore, to try and identify the practical criteria which will enable us to select, if not the best, then at least a very good structure. In order to do this we need to undertake a small diversion into the realm of the *black box*.

8.4.1 Information hiding and black boxes

Let us recall our original prospectus on behalf of structured design and composite design, on which our methodology is based. In Sec. 8.1 we stated that we assume that the user places a relatively high weighting on maintainability. What makes a structure of the type that we have been discussing highly maintainable and another, similar structure, less so?

The answer, we believe, lies with the two following statements:

- When a bug manifests itself in working software (and we know that this will always happen), its effects should be localized as far as possible. Ideally, they should be limited to the module that is the source of the bug. If they are disseminated through the structure then the resources needed to diagnose and cure the defect may become very high indeed.
- When, because of environmental or operational changes, modifications to a module need to be made, the requirement to change other modules should be minimal.

The above two statements seem to encapsulate what maintainability is all about. They imply that modules should be constructed to be as independent as possible of each other and this means that their inner workings should be secret and hidden from the other. The principle involved here is known as *information hiding* and is originally due to a software scientist named Parnas. The principle is discussed in many books dealing with design, e.g., Yourdon and Constantine (1979).

Information hiding, as described in the reference, is not all that easy to grasp. In the writer's view a more comprehensible approach is via the principle of the *black box*. This principle is discussed in any number of publications and receives a respectable treatment in Yourdon and Constantine (1979) and Page-Jones (1980). The idea of a *black box* is that it is an entity which with known inputs will provide known outputs, but its inner behaviour and structure is unknown. The principle is not restricted to software and has equally important connotations in other disciplines: electronics, medicine, social science and many others. Many of the artifacts that are around us today are black boxes to most of us. As we write this book there is a device on the desk. One input to the device enables us to receive a football match commentary. Having just satisfied ourselves that England have not been humiliated again, we have applied another input and are now listening to the Benny Goodman Quintet. The device is a cassette radio of course. But as we are sublimely ignorant of its inner circuitry, to both of us it is a black box.

There are, of course, many other items that are likely to be black boxes to many people. Probably television sets, video recorders and atom bombs are black boxes to many, computers also — but not to you, of course. To rather fewer, the internal combustion engine qualifies.

To adopt the principle of information hiding is equivalent to designing modules so that as far as possible they are black boxes to all other modules. It is generally accepted that module independence, or the degree to which they are regarded as black boxes, is a composite characteristic which depends on two other properties. One is a property of the inter-relationship between modules and is known as *coupling*. The other is a property of the modules themselves and is called *cohesion* (Yourdon and Constantine, 1979) or *strength* (Myers, 1975). We must now look at these in turn.

8.4.2 Coupling

This is defined as an abstract qualitative measure of the degree of inter-dependence between modules. In the pursuit of independence for modules the designer will aim to achieve low coupling or, adopting the terminology of the day, a clean interface. There seems to be a fair degree of agreement between designers that coupling can be represented as a spectrum of types on an ordinal scale, ranging from good to bad. By 'ordinal' we mean only that the types are ranked for desirability without any measure being attached. There is little formal basis for the categorization but a great deal of empirical evidence. Although versions vary to some extent, the following may be accepted as the spectrum of types of coupling referred to:

(a) Content coupling   Bad

(b) Common coupling

(c) Control coupling

(d) Stamp coupling

(e) Data coupling   Good

However, it must be remembered that the classification is empirically based. It has no theoretical justification, as yet. A brief description of each type follows.

(a) Content coupling Content (or pathological) coupling exists if one module refers to the inside of another. In other words, it branches into or changes data in or alters a statement in, the other module. Clearly, for this to happen the invoking module must know a great deal about the called module. With coupling of this nature the black-box concept is virtually destroyed and module indepedence goes out of the window. It is best avoided.

(b) Common coupling Modules are common coupled if they refer to the same global data. This is undesirable because, if the format of the global data needs to be changed, then many modules may be affected. Unless an up-to-date cross-reference list is maintained, which relates data items to the modules where they are used, then it may be necessary to check every module.

(c) Control coupling Two modules are control coupled if one passes a parameter to the other, with the intention of controlling its behaviour; in other words, the parameter is a flag. In general, downward-travelling flags imply that the receiving module is less than a black box. They are thus, undesirable. An example is given in Fig. 8.3.

Figure 8.3a shows a module EXEC COMMAND which is able to call another module GETCOMM. When called, GETCOMM is expected provide the parameter *Command*. However, EXEC COMMAND may require the parameter in parsed or unparsed form. The superordinate module indicates the version required by the downward-travelling parameter *Parse flag*. Thus, GETCOMM is not a black box to EXEC COMMAND.

An alternative structure, which eliminates *Parse flag* and the consequent control coupling, is shown in Fig. 8.3b. The diagram is really self-explanatory but, briefly, it shows an extra module GETPCOMM which may also call GETCOMM. EXEC COMMAND may call either GETCOMM or GETPCOMM, depending on whether it requires an unparsed or a parsed command. If *Parsed command* is required then GETPCOMM calls GETCOMM to obtain the unparsed version, parses it and returns it to EXEC COMMAND.

Upward-travelling flags, which merely report a state of affairs to a superordinate to action as it wishes, tend to be more acceptable and, indeed, inevitable.

(d) Stamp coupling Two modules are stamp coupled if they accept the same record type as a parameter. This type of coupling may manufacture interdependency between otherwise unrelated modules. An example is shown in Fig. 8.4.

A module PRODINVOICE is intended to generate invoices for car hire. The invoice value comprises two components: the basic rental charge (calculated in CALC BASECHARGE) and the mileage charge (calculated in CALC MILECHARGE). The parameter to both is *Customer record*. Now it may be that the two subordinate modules need different data items in *Customer record*. For instance, CALC BASECHARGE may need *Customer address* and *Rental period*. CALC MILECHARGE may require *Miles travelled* only. Thus a change to the format or structure of *Customer address* for the benefit of CALC BASECHARGE may enforce changes to CALC MILECHARGE. Interdependence between two apparently unrelated modules has been manufactured and they are said to be stamp coupled. A further disadvantage of this type of coupling is that it may prevent a basically simple and useful module from being used elsewhere.

(e) Data coupling If two modules communicate by parameters, each one being either a single data item or a homogeneous set of data items which do not incorporate any control element, then the modules are data coupled. This is the necessary communication between modules and is unavoidable.

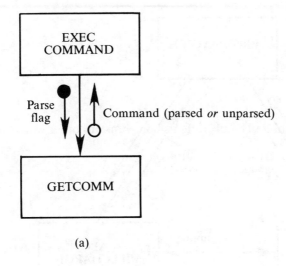

(a)

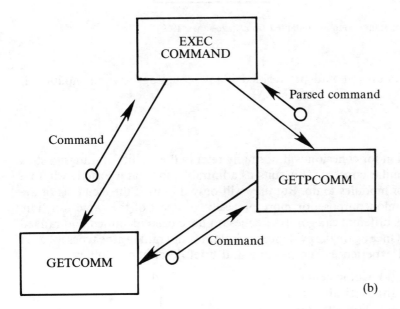

(b)

Figure 8.3 An example of control coupling and its avoidance (adapted from Myers, 1975).

The above summaries are short but we hope that they adequately convey the types of interface to be avoided if the independence of modules is to be promoted. For those wishing to take the matter further, Yourdon and Constantine (1979) and Page-Jones (1980, 2nd edn 1988) are recommended.

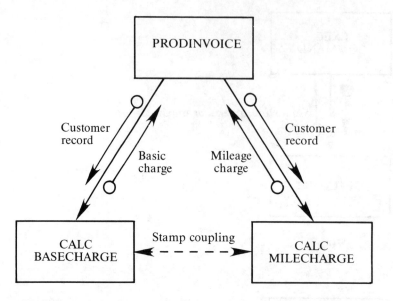

Figure 8.4 An example of stamp coupling (adapted from Page-Jones, 1980).

Exercise 8.2 What features should be avoided if low coupling between modules is to be achieved?

8.4.3 Cohesion

A dictionary definition for cohesion will normally refer to the facility of things to stick together, or some similar concept. This suits us admirably, for that is exactly what we want the elements of modules to do. But they will only do this if the elements of the module have a common purpose, or more precisely, are part of the same function.

As with coupling, different categories of cohesion have been identified and ranked on an ordinal scale. Once again the evidence for isolating and ranking the types is based mainly on practical experience. The ranking and brief descriptions follow:

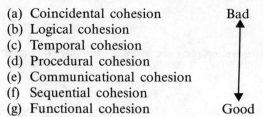

(a) Coincidental cohesion   Bad

(b) Logical cohesion

(c) Temporal cohesion

(d) Procedural cohesion

(e) Communicational cohesion

(f) Sequential cohesion

(g) Functional cohesion   Good

(a) Coincidental cohesion This occurs when there is little or no functional relationship among the elements of a module. A module that is purely coincidentally associated is a rare occurrence these days if the module is designed from scratch. It is more likely to occur as a result of trying to partition code that has already been written. Just suppose that a programmer has been instructed to attempt to partition an elderly monolithic program. Suppose also that inspection reveals a situation as shown in Fig. 8.5.

The programmer has identified a sequence of program elements that recur at random intervals in the program. The temptation is to make the sequence into a separate module which we will call X, and replace each instance of the sequence with a call to X. The elements of the new module X are not functionally related in any sense. Their presence together in X is entirely due to the coincidence of their original contiguous placement by someone long ago.

Now the inevitable happens. A bug occurs at A say, and a maintenance programmer in a hurry may cure it by changing X. But now bugs may appear at B, C, D and E, and one bug is exchanged for many. Of course, this could happen with any module with multiple calls. But experience has shown that it is much more likely to happen if the elements involved in X are not functionally related.

(b) Logical cohesion The elements of a module are logically associated if they appear to fall into the same logical class of activities. For example, we could combine into a single module all processing elements that fall into the class of getting input. e.g., read a control message from a terminal; read transactions from magnetic tape; read master records from disk. Such a module would be regarded as stronger and thus more desirable than a module in the previous class. The potential disadvantage though is that different types of input may be required at different times so that the calling module must know something about the inside of the called module and employ a downward-travelling flag into the bargain Thus the black-box concept begins to fray at the edges.

(c) Temporal cohesion The elements of a module are temporally associated if they are logically associated and related in time. An example might be an initialization module which includes such elements as: read a control message from a terminal; open disk files; reset counters; set accumulators to zero. Although temporal is regarded as stronger than logical, experience has shown that it still may lead to complications at the maintenance stage.

(d) Procedural cohesion In studies of module cohesion it was noted that if a designer used a flowchart as the basis for partitioning, the results were variable but tended to produce low-strength modules. A convincing technical explanation was difficult to derive. The main point is that if partitioning is based on procedure, in the flowchart sense, then this may well result in modules that contain parts of a number of different functions but the whole of none. An attempt to illustrate this is made in Fig. 8.6.

Part a of the diagram shows a flowchart which has been partitioned in accordance with the main procedural constructs. However, the chart relates to two separate functions, P and Q. Some of the flowchart symbols relate to one function and some to the other, as signified in the top right-hand corner of the symbols. The resulting structure chart is shown as part b. It can be seen that module C contains elements of P and Q. As B may call C, it too is regarded as multi-functional and thus not quite out of the top drawer in terms of cohesion.

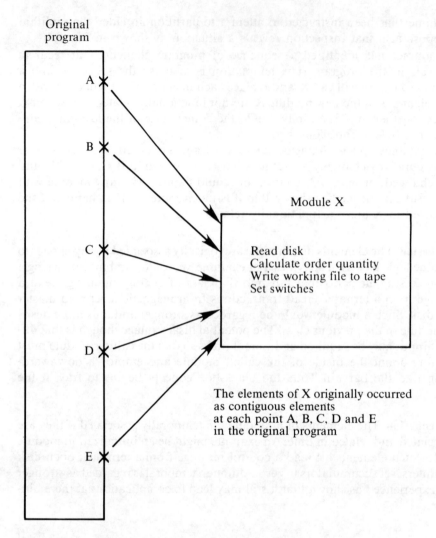

Original
program

A

B

Module X

C

Read disk
Calculate order quantity
Write working file to tape
Set switches

D

The elements of X originally occurred
as contiguous elements
at each point A, B, C, D and E
in the original program

E

Figure 8.5 An example of coincidental cohesion.

(e) Communicational cohesion This type of cohesion occurs when the elements of the module use the same input data or contribute to the same output data. This type of cohesion is best illustrated by means of a dataflow diagram, Fig. 8.7.

The diagram shows the same dataflow, *Gross pay*, entering three transforms in parallel, *Calculate net pay, Calculate average gross pay* and *Update project costs*. If these three transforms are combined into the single module, USEGROSS, then it would be communicational. On the whole, such modules are acceptable although experience has shown that they may on occasion cause maintenance problems.

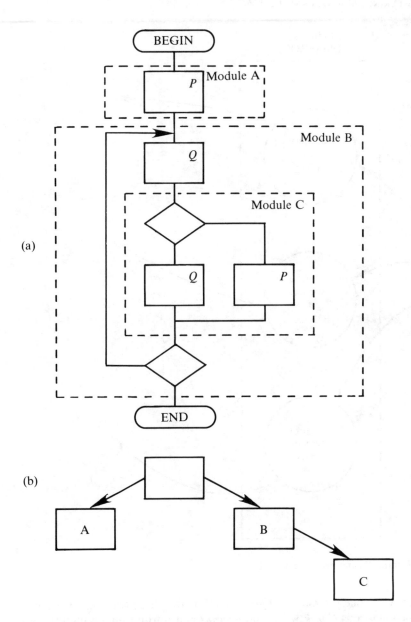

(a)

(b)

Figure 8.6 Flowchart procedure leading to procedural cohesion.

(f) Sequential cohesion With this type, the output data from one element serves as input to another. Once again this type is best illustrated by a dataflow diagram, Fig. 8.8.

The diagram shows a data item, *Quantity I* proceeding through a series of three different checks. The partially checked versions are labelled *Quantity II* and *Quantity III*,

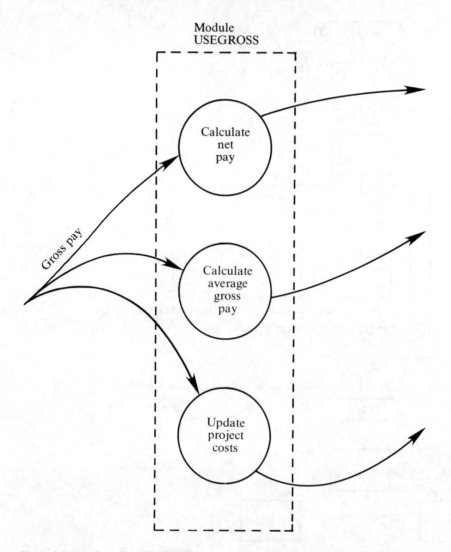

Figure 8.7 Dataflow diagram illustrating communicational cohesion.

respectively. The fully checked version is *Quantity IV*. If the three transforms shown, *Check format, Check range* and *Check validity* are combined into the module CHECK-QUANT, then such a module would be sequentially cohesive. As such a partitioning approach may result in the inclusion of part-functions into a single module, rather than one complete function, it is not regarded as the ultimate, cohesion-wise.

(g) Functional cohesion In a completely functional module, every element is an integral part of, and is essential to, the performance of a *single function*. A good operational definition is the following: 'If it is not sequential, communicational, procedural, temporal, logical or coincidential ... then it is functional!'

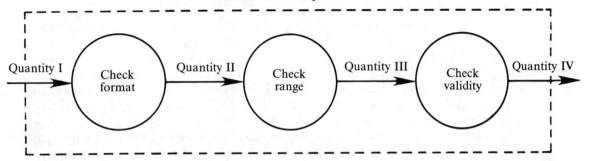

Figure 8.8 Dataflow diagram illustrating sequential cohesion.

The above is sufficient to convey the flavour of the concept of cohesion. As in the previous section, the references there given will provide a more detailed treatment for those who wish to take the matter further.

Exercise 8.3 The following is a list of modules with a brief indication of what they are expected to do. Rank them in order of decreasing cohesiveness.

A — calculates tax and net pay
B — opens a file and initializes an array
C — calculates the date of Easter for every year between 1990 and 2001 AD
D — calculates the date of Easter 1995 and prints it out

8.4.4 Summary

We have examined the question of evaluating partitioning from the premise that the independence of modules from each other is of prime importance. We noted that this quality of independence is a composite of two other properties, coupling and cohesion. In order to achieve low coupling it is essential to design clean, simple interfaces between modules. Good cohesion is a feature of modules wherein all elements are devoted to the performance of a single function.

As you would probably expect, low coupling between modules usually implies that they are highly cohesive, and vice versa. But the two characteristics are not always perfectly correlated in this way. Where a conflict is experienced between the two, it is generally reckoned that cohesion is the more important, so that this should be borne in mind at the initial design stage.

8.5 DESIGN STRATEGY

So far, we have theorized at some length on modules, their inter-relationships and the features that distinguish the good from the bad. We have not, as yet, said anything about actually doing design, an omission that must be repaired without further delay.

Remember that, in theory, we should be generating all possible designs and choosing the best. But, for a reason discussed in Chapter 7 we know that this is quite impossible. Let us remind you why this is. It is the question of size of selection. The number of possible designs is so huge that it is quite impossible to examine them all.

We must expect therefore, that our answer to the size of selection problem, namely design heuristics, will begin to play an important part in our design activities. A recommended formal procedure using heuristics, which will allow us to move swiftly to a good first design, is known as a *design strategy*. We shall examine two such strategies. The first of these may be regarded as the most important of the structured design approaches. This will be considered in fair detail. The second is regarded as a little less important and as it has much in common with the first, it will receive rather less attention.

8.5.1 Transform-centred design

This, the primary structured design strategy, consists of four stages, but as we shall see we are in the fortunate position of being able to ignore the first. The stages are:

(a) Re-state the specification as a dataflow diagram (DFD).
(b) Identify the central transforms.
(c) Factor to the first level.
(d) Factor the afferent, efferent and transform branches.

We can rapidly dispose of (a). As we used dataflow techniques at the analysis stage our specifications will include DFDs anyway, and it so happens that the DeMarco style of analysis provides outputs that are ideal for the purpose. We shall look at the other stages in turn, but before we do so we must say a few words more about modules.

Module classes   In terms of the role that they play in a structure there are four basic classes of module and these are illustrated in Fig. 8.9.

Diagram a of Fig. 8.9 shows a module that obtains data from a subordinate and passes it up to a superordinate. In this case, the module also effects a transformation on the data, converting it from x to y. Such a flow pattern is referred to as *afferent flow* and the module is classified as an *afferent module*. The word *afferent* is a strange one to the ears of most computer people. It comes from the world of physiology where afferent neurons carry sensory data from the bodily extremities towards the brain, or so we are told. Such a module would most probably be involved in inputting data to the software and the use of the word afferent avoids the need to use the rather overworked term, input.

The counterpart to the above is illustrated in diagram b. In this case the module takes data item x from its superordinate, changes it to y and passes it to a subordinate. This pattern is most likely to be involved in output and we refer to *efferent flow* and *efferent module*. The physiological reference here is to the efferent nerves which carry motor signals from the brain to the limbs.

Some modules exist purely to transform data into some other form. Diagram c illustrates such a module. Data item x is received from a superordinate, it is converted to y and passed back. *Transform flow* and *transform module* are the appropriate terms here.

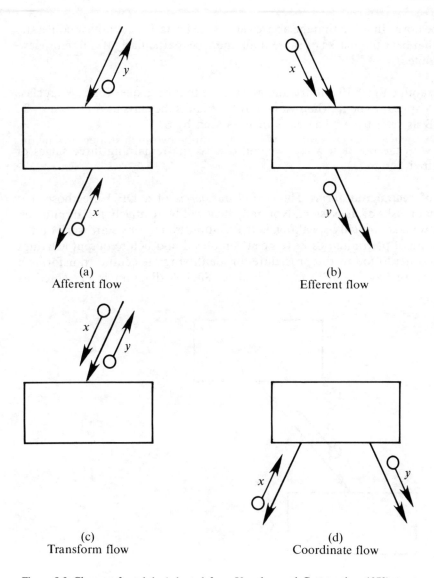

Figure 8.9 Classes of module (adapted from Yourdon and Constantine, 1979).

Most of the computational work in a typical system would take place within such modules.

Finally, some modules have a busy-body type of function. Their life is spent in interfering in the affairs of others, or more diplomatically, they have a managerial role. Such modules appear, frequently but not exclusively, fairly high in the software structure and an example is shown in diagram d. Here, the *coordinate module* supervises two subordinates, receives data item *x* from one of them and dispatches data item *y* to the other.

It should be borne in mind that the above classes are basic. Frequently, modules are encountered that bear the marks of more than one type, particularly if different view-points are adopted.

Exercise 8.4 Examine Fig. 8.10 and try and answer the following questions: What class does module A appear to be in when viewed by S? What is the class of A as seen by T? The class of B as seen by A? The class of B as seen by S?

We are now in the position where we can discuss the remaining three stages of transform-centred design.

Identification of central transforms The *central transforms* of a DFD are those that perform the main tasks of the system. Normally they will be relatively few in number. The view that we take, roughly speaking, is that central transforms start work on the data when the input preliminaries have been completed and before output activities commence. In order to follow the procedure for identifying the central transforms it is essential that we have a DFD to manipulate. Such a diagram is presented as Fig. 8.11.

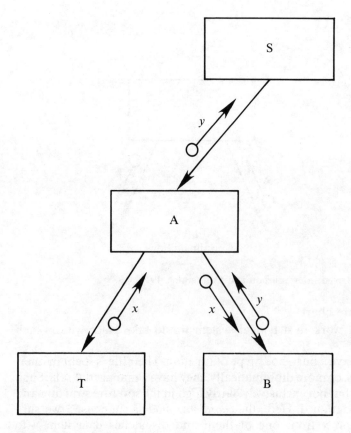

Figure 8.10 A combination of modules.

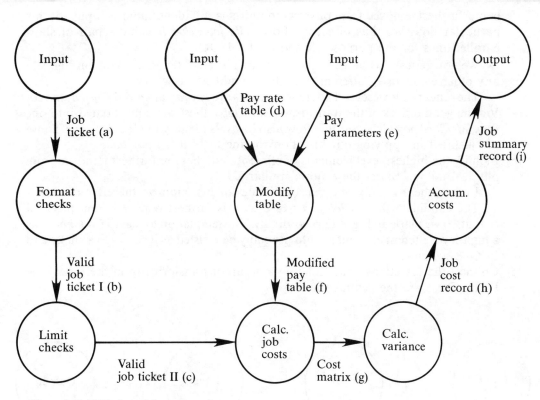

Figure 8.11 DFD for a job-costing scheme.

Briefly, the diagram represents part of a costing procedure whereby pay rates are applied to job tickets (transactions representing the hours worked by individual workers on different jobs) to derive job costs. Variances, which are merely the difference between actual and predicted costs, are calculated and a job summary record is output. And that is all that you need to know at this stage about the inner working of the procedure. What is important, but should be clear from the DFD, is that there are three different inputs: the job tickets themselves, a table of pay rates and pay parameters that are used to modify the table. There is only one output, the job summary record. Just note that the dataflows are labelled properly with their names but we have added a code, in the form of a lower case alphabetic character, as well. This is just to make life easier when we develop the structure chart.

We now follow a standard procedure:

(a) <u>Identify the highest level elements of afferent data that are furthest removed from physical input yet are still identifiable as inputs to the system. Bisect the flows representing these elements.</u> If we follow the flow of *Job ticket* we note that it is successively transformed into *Valid job ticket I* and *Valid job ticket II*. There seems to be a case for assuming that this particular afferent flow loses its individuality once it enters the transform *Calc. job costs*. Consequently, we regard *Valid job ticket II* as being 'furthest removed from physical input yet is still identifiable as input' for this particular flow. We thus bisect the flow *Valid job ticket II* using a pair of short parallel lines for the purpose, as shown in Fig. 8.12.

We now repeat this procedure for the other afferent flows, marking on Fig. 8.12 any other elements of afferent data that should be bisected.

The other two lowest level afferent elements are *Pay rate table* and *Pay parameters*. Via the good offices of the transform *Modify table* these are consolidated into one flow, *Modified pay table*. But this flow also loses its identity in *Calc. job costs*. So we are justified in applying our bisection routine to *Modified pay table*.

(b) Identify the highest level elements of efferent data that are furthest removed from physical output. Bisect these flows similarly.

In fact, there is only one real candidate for bisection on the efferent side.

The candidate flow is *Job cost record* as it is furthest removed from physical output, so we mark up Fig. 8.12 accordingly. The temptation to regard *Cost matrix* as a high-level efferent element should probably be resisted as it comes to a sticky end in *Calc. variance*.

(c) Connect the bisections, thus isolating a group of transforms from the rest of the DFD. These are the central transforms.

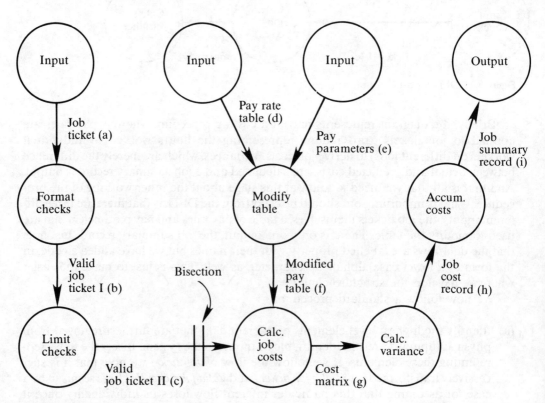

Figure 8.12 DFD with bisected afferent flow.

As the result of our activities in the previous part the amended version of Fig. 8.12 should now show the double-line bisection symbol on three flows: *Valid job ticket II, Modified pay table* and *Job cost record.* If you now look at Fig. 8.13 you will see the bisection symbols in place and a dashed line joining them and enclosing the central transforms, *Calc. job costs* and *Calc. variance.*

We must emphasise at this stage that this part of the procedure is subjective. You may well have rebelled during our application of the procedure and insisted that *Modified pay table* is not really an afferent flow at all. In which case you would have ended up with a different set of central transforms.

As you would have had to push this particular bisection back towards physical input you would have *Bisected pay rate table* together with *Pay parameters* instead. Therefore, you would have acquired a set of three central transforms: *Calc. job costs, Calc. variance* and *Modify table.*

It is quite in order for you to do this as it is for any group of designers to differ at this stage of the design process. Very often design is not just a matter of making a choice between black and white. Shades of grey are involved and maybe that is what makes it, to us anyway, the most fascinating of the life cycle phases. But for the moment we shall

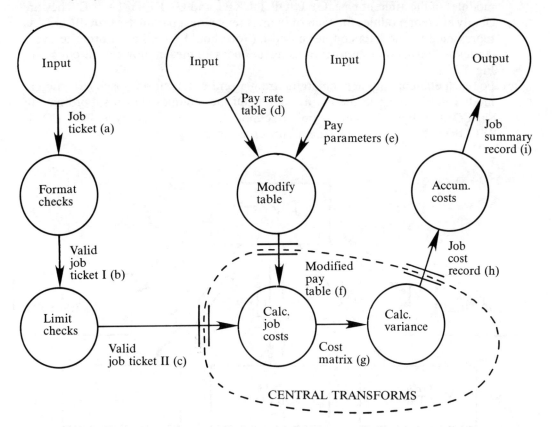

Figure 8.13 DFD showing central transforms.

assume that we were all in complete agreement on our interpretation of this particular DFD and we shall proceed to complete our first-cut design.

First level factoring The term *factoring* is really just another term for partitioning. This stage is quite straightforward and leaves little room for manoeuvre on the part of the designer. Three simple actions are called for:

(a) Establish a main module. Viewed from above, as if by a user or supervisory program, this module *is* the software. Hence, it is helpful to name it accordingly. We will name the module JOBCOST and show it at the apex of the sketch given as Fig. 8.14.

 Although JOBCOST will appear to be carrying out the function entirely on its own, it will in fact do so by employing subordinate modules. So that the remaining three stages are concerned with establishing JOBCOST's view of who the subordinates are.

(b) For each afferent data item entering one or more central transforms, specify an afferent module in a subordinate capacity to the main module.

 Of the modules shown subordinate to JOBCOST in Fig. 8.14 there are two modules of the afferent type, GET JOB TICKET and GET PAY TABLE. They are clearly afferent modules for each of them is returning a parameter to JOBCOST as represented by the data couples c and f. (You should note that in order to avoid clutter on the diagram we are now using the codes for the dataflows as introduced in Fig. 8.11.)

(c) For each efferent data item emerging from a central transform, specify an efferent module subordinate to the main module. Of the modules shown subordinate to JOBCOST in Fig. 8.14 there is only one module of the efferent type, PUT COST RECORD. The efferent data item concerned is h.

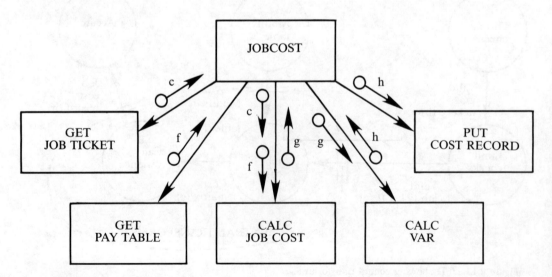

Figure 8.14 First level factoring of JOBCOST.

(d) For each central transform, specify a subordinate transform module.

The two modules in question are CALC JOB COST and CALC VAR. and these may be recognized immediately as belonging to the class of transform modules. CALC JOB COST receives the data couples c and f from its superordinate JOBCOST, derives g, and returns it. Similarly, CALC VAR receives g and returns h.

First level factoring is now complete. We have established five modules that are directly subordinate to JOBCOST. Two of these are of the afferent type, one is efferent and the remaining two are transform. So we have, in effect, sprouted three different types of *branch*, each one of which is classified by the type of module at its root. We have two afferent, one efferent and two transform branches. We must now do our best to factor these branches further.

Factoring of afferent, efferent and transform branches Convention seems to demand that the afferent branches should be tackled first although there is no reason why the sequence cannot be changed if you so desire. However, we will be conventional and elect to factor down one of the afferent branches, the one rooted in GET JOB TICKET. The task of GET JOB TICKET is to supply c to JOBCOST. However, c must be produced from something and to find out what that something is we must return to the dataflow diagram. Figure 8.11, 8.12 or 8.13 will tell us what we want to know. We note that c is derived from b by means of the transform *Limit checks*. This indicates to us that GET JOB TICKET has a double role: a getting-input role and a transform role. So it seems sensible to give GET JOB TICKET two subordinates: an afferent module, GET FORM, and a transform module, CHECK LIMITS. This first stage of factoring GET JOB TICKET is shown as Fig. 8.15.

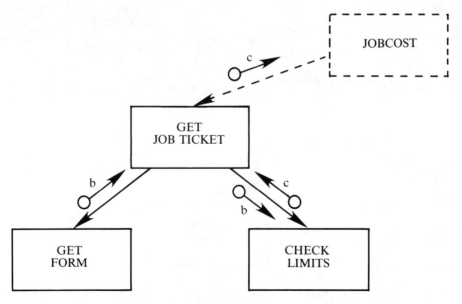

Figure 8.15 Factoring of GET JOB TICKET — first stage.

There is not much further to go. We leave CHECK LIMITS alone. But GET FORM is in much the same position now as GET JOB TICKET was initially. It needs to pass up b, and b needs to be derived from something. The DFD tells us that the something is a and, consequently GET FORM requires an afferent subordinate and a transform subordinate and these are shown in Fig. 8.16.

The diagram shows that the afferent subordinate GET INPUT provides a, while the transform subordinate CHECK FORMAT converts a into b. We have now reached physical input and need proceed no further.

We now attempt to factor GET PAY TABLE using the above method. The factoring of GET PAY TABLE introduces a minor complication. We know from Fig. 8.14 that the role of this module is to provide f to JOBCOST. We check with the DFD and note that f is derived from dataflows d and e via the transform *Modify table*. So, clearly, GET PAY TABLE needs a transform subordinate and not one but *two* afferent subordinates. This factoring is displayed in Fig. 8.17.

The figure shows the two afferent modules, GET TABLE and GET PARAS, which provide d and e, respectively. The transform subordinate MOD TABLE does the hard work of converting d and e into f. We are back to physical input for each of the constituent flows, so that factoring of this particular branch ends here.

In tackling the efferent branch we take a similar approach, factoring each efferent module into subordinate transform and further efferent modules. Appropriate factoring is shown in Fig. 8.18.

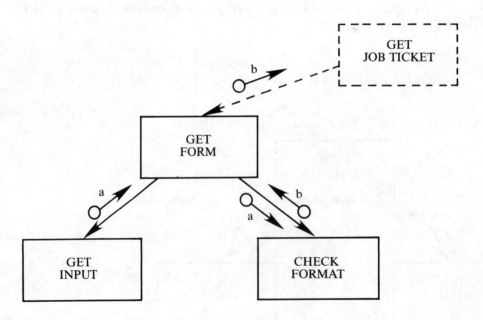

Figure 8.16 Factoring of GET JOB TICKET — second stage.

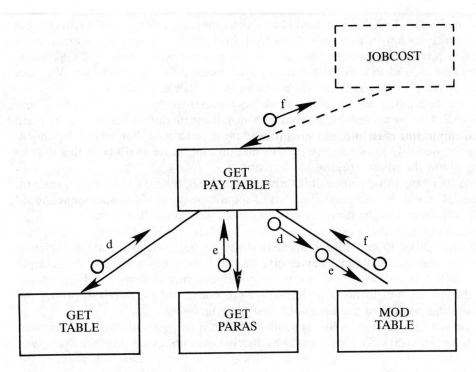

Figure 8.17 Factoring of GET PAY TABLE.

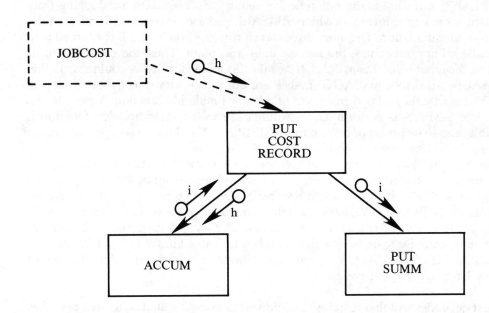

Figure 8.18 Factoring of PUT COST RECORD.

The module PUT COST RECORD has a clear transform role as well as an efferent one, for it receives h which we know from the DFD must be changed to i before it takes the road to physical output. Accordingly, we show two subordinates: ACCUM which derives i from h, and PUT SUMM which passes i on. At this point we stop. We have reached physical output and can do no more to the efferent branch.

We now turn to the two transform branches represented by CALC JOB COST and CALC VAR. Can we do anything about factoring these modules? The answer is plain 'no' — as far as our current job costing procedure is concerned. For we are dependent entirely on the DFD as our source of information and, as we well know, this tells us nothing about the inner workings of transforms.

But is there any other source of information that might help us to factor transform branches? There is. It is the Specification of requirements. For this document should include transform specifications or mini-specs as we have called them.

Consequently, at this point in real life a designer would delve deeply into this document in order to convince himself that the central transforms are sufficiently cohesive to remain unfactored. Perversely, we will have a quick look at an example where central transform *names* alone provide a clue to further factoring. Figure 8.19a shows the central transforms of a simulation procedure and Fig. 8.19b illustrates the corresponding portion of the results of first level factoring.

A computer simulation of this type involves the manipulation of a mathematical model of a process. SIMSYS appears to be conceived as a computer program that, given certain inputs, will provide a forecast of sales of a product and an indication of the necessary manufacturing arrangements. Close examination of the names given to the transform modules indicates that they appear to fall into two classes: a class that consists of SIMSALES alone and a class comprising SIMMACH, SIMLINE and AGGPLANT. But what is the rationale for making this classification? Judging from transform names, transform 5 on which SIMSALES is based is concerned with the sales aspects of the simulation. The other three transforms, 6, 8 and 9, are all concerned with physical facilities: machines, production lines and plant. Thus, the classification is based on the function of the modules. If we take this a little further we could reason that SIMMACH, SIMLINE and AGGPLANT are not satisfactory direct subordinates to SIMSYS because they all perform a part of a major simulation function. A module that appears to SIMSYS as performing the whole of this facilities simulation function is desirable, and so we invent one. We name it SIMPLANT and the revised partitioning of the transform branches is shown in Fig. 8.20.

The example illustrates that sometimes transform names from the DFD will help in factoring the transform branches. But, of course, this is no substitute for the appropriate mini-specs which must be consulted eventually. Let us return then to the transform branches of JOBCOST. We have no other source of information than the DFD. However, the names of the associated transforms, *Calc. job costs* and *Calc. variance* sound pretty cohesive to us, so we will not make a fuss about it. We will just assume that CALC JOB COST and CALC VAR are worthy modules as they stand. And this means that we have our first-cut design.

The first-cut design   All that remains to be done is to assemble all the factored branches into one diagram and we will then have the structure chart for this design, Fig. 8.21.

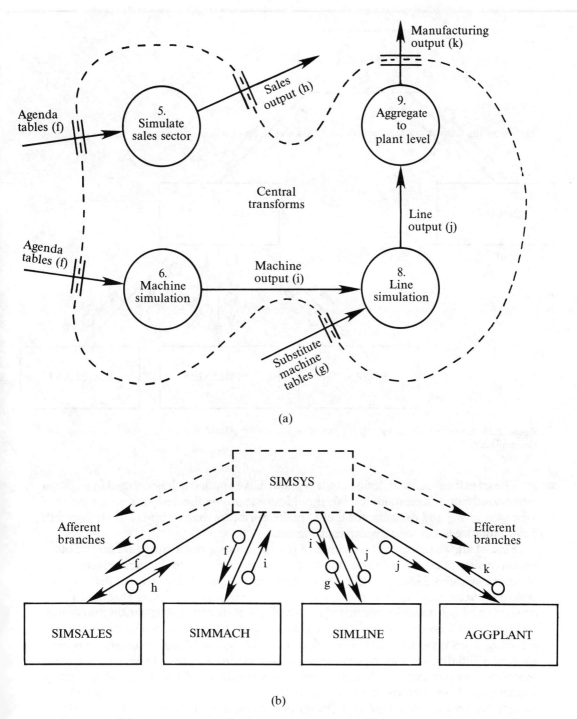

(a)

(b)

Figure 8.19 Central transforms and transform branches of SIMSYS (adapted from Yourdon and Constantine, 1979).

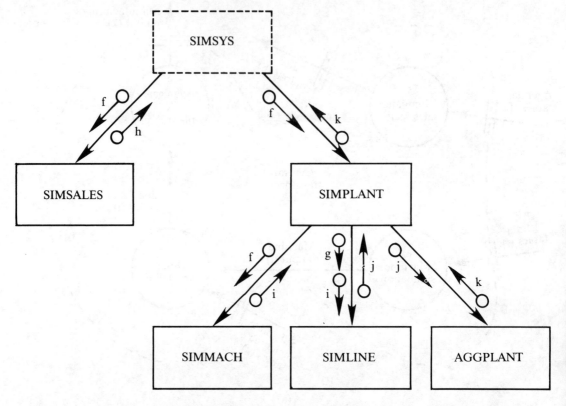

Figure 8.20 Attempted factoring of transform branches of SIMSYS (adapted from Yourdon and Constantine, 1979).

The transform-centred design strategy, as we have applied it, has resulted in a system partitioned into fifteen modules. We should now examine the design from the point of view of *coupling* and *cohesion,* for these are the attributes that we hope our strategy will have enhanced. Let us consider *coupling* first.

First of all, we perceive no evidence of *content coupling* in our structure for the inter-faces consist entirely of parameter passing with no references to the inner mechanisms of called modules. Neither is there any reference to a global data area so that we may regard *common coupling* as non-existent also. There is also a complete absence of both upward- and downward-travelling flags which indicates to us that there is no *control coupling* built into our design. (In passing, we note that the absence of downward-travelling flags provides a broad hint that the introduction of *logical cohesion* has been avoided.) Finally, we may observe that no two modules appear to receive the same record type as parameter so that no unnecessary interdependence in the form of *stamp coupling* has been manufactured. We are left with the pervasive *data coupling* which is acceptable and, as indicated in a previous section, is unavoidable.

In trying to assess the structure from the point of view of *cohesion* we are on less safe ground than previously, for we are now concerned with the inner workings of the

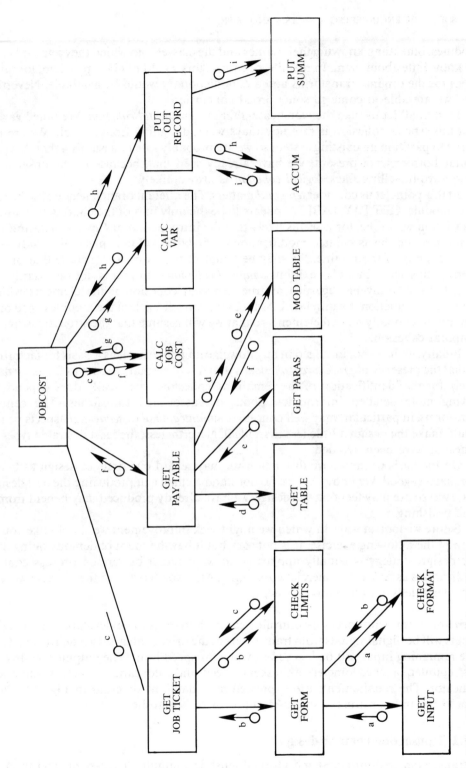

Figure 8.21 Structure chart for JOBCOST.

modules; other than knowing their names and the classes into which they appear to fall, we know little about them. In real life, of course, this would not be a problem, for mini-specs for the original transforms and a data dictionary would be available. Nevertheless, we are able to come to some broad conclusions.

First of all let us take the worst case, that of *coincidental cohesion*. We noted earlier that this type of cohesion is rare nowadays when designing from scratch. We are not trying to partition an existing system so we are probably safe in assuming that this particular horror is not present. We have already seen that, because of the absence of downward-travelling flags, *logical cohesion* is also unlikely.

At this point let us consider *temporal* matters. The afferent branch headed by the first level module, GET PAY TABLE, appears to be the only part of the chart with a strong association with time, for it seems likely that the introduction of *Pay rate table* and *Pay parameters* and the associated modification of the table will take place once only — at the beginning of the routine. We may be tempted, therefore, to conclude that one or more of this set of modules exhibits *temporal cohesion*. But this is not necessarily the case. It would only be regarded as true temporal cohesion if the elements within modules are functionally unrelated. As far as we can tell, each of the modules need only contain functionally related elements so that we will assume that the structure is free of temporal cohesion.

Finally, we have not indulged in any flowcharting nor used it as a basis for factoring, so that the presence of *procedural cohesion* is unlikely. And that is about as far as we dare to go, for the identification of the remaining cohesion types really does depend on having more detailed information about the associated transforms. The central transforms, in particular, may well conceal *communicational* or *sequential* aspects which would make the design a little less than ideal. Nevertheless, the least desirable types of cohesion have been avoided.

On the basis of the above discussion we may regard our first-cut design as being adequate-to-good. We know that we do not stand a chance of producing the best design but, even so, we may feel that the design we have already produced may benefit from a little polishing.

Before we look at ways in which we might seek improvement we should like you to attempt the following exercise. It is not easy but it has the merit of demonstrating that our design strategy is equally applicable to what might be termed process control applications as it is to commercial computing. After you have tried the exercise we will consider briefly an alternative strategy.

Exercise 8.5 A microprocessor-controlled car dashboard is to be developed. Two of the inputs will be digital signals from transducers at the drive shaft and fuel delivery system. The remaining input will be a keyed-in value for speed limit. The outputs will drive a rev. counter, a speedometer, an excess speed indicator and a fuel-consumption indicator. The requirements are expressed as a dataflow diagram in Fig. 8.22. You should try and construct a structure chart for the controller.

8.5.2 Transaction-centred design

'A transaction, in its broadest, most formal sense, is a stimulus to a system that triggers a

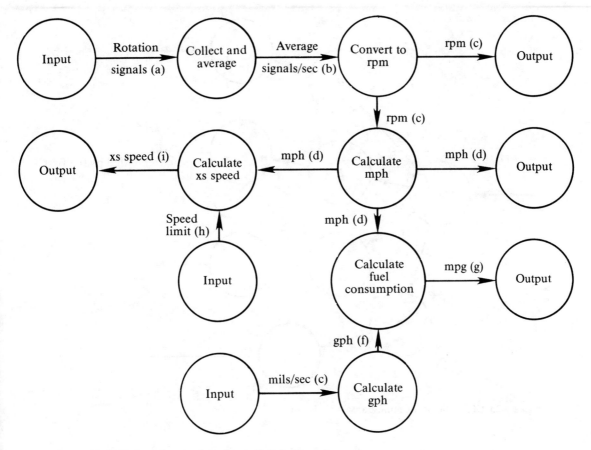

Figure 8.22 DFD for microprocessor-controlled dashboard.

set of activities within the system. Examples of transactions or a signal to a space vehicle to fire its retro engines, a coolant-temperature alarm in a fission reactor, or a clock interrupt in an operating system. The activities associated with these transactions would be, respectively, the firing of the space vehicle's retro engines, the shutting down of the reactor, and the starting of a new time slice' (Page-Jones, 1980).

The above definition has certain implications for dataflow diagrams. If a dataflow comprizes a number of transactions, each calling for a series of activities, then we can predict that a certain pattern-type will appear in the DFD, and an example is given in Fig. 8.23.

We can see a dataflow x entering a transform X which splits it into several discrete output streams, a, b, c and d. Each of the discrete streams gets involved with its own set of transforms such as A, B, C and D, etc. If such a pattern is encountered it is worth considering the application of transaction-centred design strategy, which may be summarized as follows:

(a) Specify a *transaction centre*. This is a module that should be responsible for getting

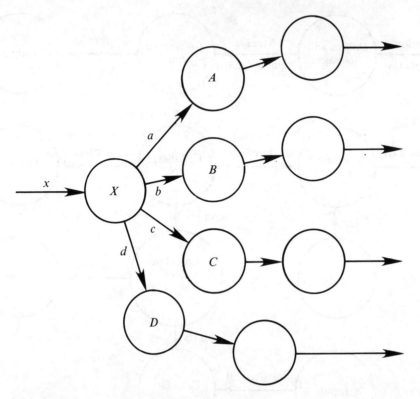

Figure 8.23 DFD pattern for multi-transaction handling.

the dataflow, analysing each transaction to determine its type and dispatching it to the appropriate subordinate for processing.

(b) For each transaction type specify a transaction module, subordinate to the transaction centre, to process it.

(c) Factor each transaction module down as far as is necessary to ensure that each processing branch consists of modules that are as cohesive as possible.

The application of the strategy means that the structure chart for Fig. 8.23 would take on the general appearances of the one shown in Fig. 8.24.

Note that the construction of Fig. 8.24 entails the use of a new symbol. The rectangle with a diamond inserted in its lower margin is the symbol for a transaction centre. The equivalent of first level factoring has resulted in a subordinate module GETFLOW which is of the afferent class and provides the stream of transactions to be analysed on type by CENTREX. The other subordinates, TRANSONE, TRANSTWO, TRANSTHREE and TRANSFOUR, are intended to be responsible for the processing of *a, b, c* and *d* respectively. We would expect each of these transaction modules to be superordinate to other, lower-level modules.

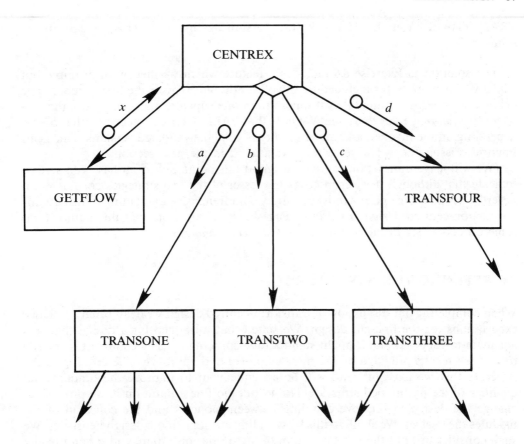

Figure 8.24 Structure chart for multi-transaction handling.

You may wish to demand a halt at this point and register a protest. You may have encountered transaction-processing systems where the processing of some transaction types differed only in some small degree. An example would be a case where a number of transaction types are subjected to comprehensive and largely identical validity checking before they are involved in unique and relatively small-scale updating, say. You would like to point out that the result of using this strategy in such circumstances would appear to be an eventual implementation in which large amounts of program code are duplicated, triplicated or worse. This is a distinct possibility of course, but the state of affairs can often be avoided. Let us imagine that *b* and *c* are to be subjected to virtually identical validation checks. If the common element can be regarded as functionally cohesive, there is no reason why it cannot be extracted as a separate module which is made subordinate to *both* TRANSTWO and TRANSTHREE.

Exercise 8.6 Re-draw Fig. 8.24 using the assumption that a functionally cohesive module **VALIDCHECK** can be specified which may be invoked by both TRANSTWO and

TRANSTHREE. You should check your version against ours. This appears in the solution.

The solution to Exercise 8.6 includes a feature which we met in an example but which we have not so far included in any of our designs. This is the first time we have deliberately specified a module with more than one superordinate. Or, to use the vernacular, a *fan-in* greater than one. We note that VALIDCHECK receives either b or c, depending on the invoker, and returns either b^0 or c^0 the validated versions. This is an important issue and will receive fuller treatment in the next section.

(We will leave transaction-centred design at this point. Sufficient has been said to indicate that although it is regarded as the lesser of the two strategies considered, it nevertheless has some points in its favour. A comprehensive and enthusiastic case for transaction-centred design is made in Page-Jones, 1980). Note that this author (and some others) refers to the technique as *transaction analysis*.

8.6 REFINING THE STRUCTURE

When completing our discussion of transform-centred design we dealt briefly with our expectations for the first-cut design. We stated that we hoped for a design that was adequate-to-good but that it might stand a little sprucing up. The comment is equally true of the results provided by the transaction-centred approach. The refining of the structure that we have in mind will be an endeavour to improve the fundamental qualities of the partitioned structure. Not to put too fine a point on it, we propose to change the design to improve coupling between modules and the cohesion of the modules themselves. We shall do this by wheeling out some more design heuristics. We shall consider three of the most common of these rules-of-thumb, and try and justify their use. When we first introduced the idea of heuristics in Chapter 7 we mentioned that they are rather like public-house pontifications with built-in quotation marks. We shall pursue this refreshing analogy to the extent of printing each heuristic in italics and in quotes, before embarking on the associated discussion.

8.6.1 Module size

'A module should contain between 10 and 100 statements'

We immediately note a problem. As the design has not been implemented, or even designed in detail, how do we know how many statements are included in a module? Well, we do not. It may be of course that, on the basis of the DFD and mini-specs, the designer may be able to make an educated guess. Such a guess is more easily made at the detailed design stage, as we shall see in Chapter 9. So we may find this particular rule applied later in the design phase, with any module failing the test initiating a temporary return to initial design.

The rationale for this rule is simple. Experience has shown that if a module contains more than 100 statements then error correction becomes most uneconomic. At the other end of the scale, modules that are less than ten statements in length are inefficient, for the non-productive overhead involved in calling them tends to overshadow whatever advantages they entail. To some extent small modules become more respectable when they have a high *fan-in*. In other words, if they make themselves thoroughly useful by avoiding areas of replicated code, then their operational deficiencies may be forgiven.

Within the 10 to 100 range you will find some optimal figures proposed. A favourite number is 50 — because that is the number of statements that fits nicely on one page of listing paper. It is thus seen as a convenient size and format for a maintenance programmer to work from. On the other hand, others advocate 30 as the magic number. Research has shown that a programmer's comprehension of a module's functionality drops dramatically beyond this point (Weinberg, 1970).

We should not make too much of an issue of module size. As has been said: 'It is possible (though unlikely) that there exists a single self-contained function which is only sensibly realized as a 2000 statement FORTRAN subroutine' (Yourdon and Constantine, 1979). It makes no sense to cut such a module up into arbitrary pieces just to play the numbers game. The correct approach should be to at least examine critically any module that offends the size guidelines. Any corrective action should be contingent upon its overall effect on cohesion and coupling.

For example, given that in the course of refining a design you estimate that a module is not only too big but also logically cohesive, what action would you take? In this case there is a good chance that such a module combines two or more functions. The ploy is, therefore, to return to the structure chart and see if the very large module may be factored further.

As another example, if you encounter a very small module with a fan-in of one, and so is clearly not earning its keep, what action would you suggest? The situation we have in mind is illustrated in Fig. 8.25.

SMALLMOD is a very small module subordinate to A and superordinate to B. The only real chance of eliminating SMALLMOD is either to compress it upwards so that it combines with A, or compress it downwards so that it combines with B. These alternatives are displayed in Fig. 8.26.

Clearly, if neither of these alternatives may be taken without upsetting the properties of the host module, then we just have to accept that SMALLMOD is there to stay.

8.6.2 Fan-out

'The fan-out of a module should be less than 8'

This is a feature of modules so far unmentioned. *Fan-out* is directly discernible from the structure chart and is defined as the number of direct subordinates of a module. If this number is excessive the module is deemed as likely to be too complex for comfort and correspondingly difficult to maintain. The origin of the upper limit of eight is obscure. It is at least partially based on Miller's 'magical number seven, plus or minus two'. This is all about the limits of human capacity for processing information. It is often quoted as evidence of the number of subordinates that a human manager can cope with efficiently. It is interesting, therefore, that a heuristic that won its spurs in the field of human organization design is now quoted in the context of software design.

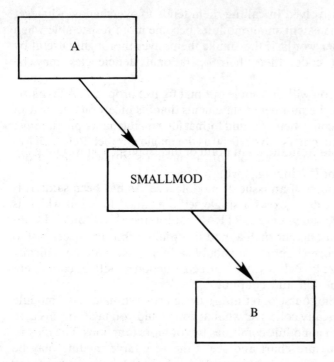

Figure 8.25 Structure chart incorporating SMALLMOD.

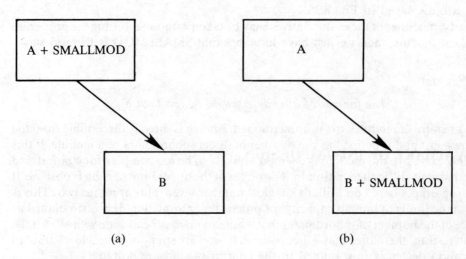

(a)   (b)

Figure 8.26 Elimination of SMALLMOD.

Once again, we handle the rule with care. We are merely saying that if the number of direct subordinates of a module does exceed eight, then it warrants critical study. Frequently such high fan-outs are evidence of failure to define intermediate levels of module. To emphasize this point we should like you to try the following exercise.

Exercise 8.7 Figure 8.27 represents the structure chart for a first-cut design. In order to compensate for the lack of requirements documentation, we have been more than usually informative in titling the modules. We have not included any data couples as we do not wish you to be distracted from the main point of the exercise. You will note that the top module (and the system) is named COMPUTE NET PAY. We should like you to try and reduce the fan-out of COMPUTE NET PAY by introducing some intermediate modules into the structure.

8.6.3 Fan-in

'Fan-in should be maximized — but not at any cost'

We have already hymned the praises of high fan-in in the context of the very small module. But it is an agreeable feature for any size of module. It represents the elimination of replicated code and, thus, is highly desirable from the maintenance point of view. The one caution that we must emphasize relates to the second part of the definition. It is fundamentally wrong to squeeze out some function from a number of potential superordinates and call it a module, if the function is not truly common. The result will be a less-than-clean interface with each calling module involving downward-travelling flags and so on.

8.6.4 Summary

We have introduced three of the more common and more useful design heuristics which may be used to refine a first-cut design. There are many others of course, but on the whole their use is a little more delicate and should be deferred until some experience of initial design is acquired. Reasonable accounts of the possibilities in this area are to be found in Page-Jones (1980) and Yourdon and Constantine (1979).

A final statement is in order. We have been discussing heuristics and not dogma, despite the man in the local drinking establishment. Heuristics can be very valuable if used properly. They can lead to computing disasters if they are not.

8.7 SUMMARY OF INITIAL DESIGN

In this chapter we have devoted our attention to designing an intial structure for the software that we want to build, starting from a dataflow diagram. Also, via the concepts of coupling and cohesion, we have highlighted the features that will distinguish a good design from the mediocre or downright bad. We then examined two strategies, one common and one less so, that will usually allow us to arrive at a reasonable design fairly quickly. Finally, on the understanding that our first-cut design will stand some

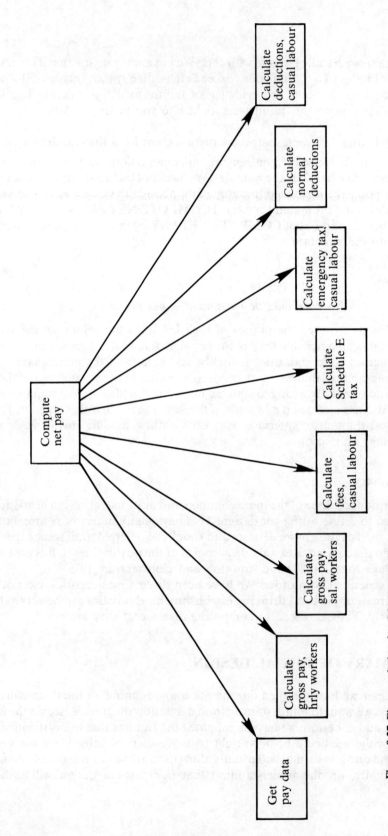

Figure 8.27 First-cut design for COMPUTE NET PAY.

92

improvement, we discussed some simple rules-of-thumb to achieve this refinement. But the modules that we have identified at this stage are still largely black boxes to us, as well as each other. So we must now put some flesh on the skeleton and consider the question of detailed design.

REFERENCES

Myers, G. J. (1975) *Reliable Software through Composite Design*, Van Nostrand Reinhold, Wokingham.

Page-Jones, M. (1980) *The Practical Guide to Structured System Design*, Yourdon Press, New York. (2nd edn, 1988)

Weinberg, G. M. (1970) *PL/1 Programming: a Manual of Style*, McGraw-Hill, New York.

Yourdon, E. and Constantine, L. L. (1979) *Structured Design: Fundamentals of a Discipline of Computer Program and System Design*, Prentice-Hall, Englewood Cliffs, New Jersey.

9

DETAILED DESIGN

9.1 INTRODUCTION

By way of a design strategy, such as those discussed in Chapter 8, we arrive at the structure of a fairly good design. By dint of applying design heuristics, as discussed in the same chapter, we improve it until, modest to a fault, we announce that we now have a good design. Our cohesion is functional; our interfaces are clean. Why do not we package the structure chart up with the mini-specs and the data dictionary and turn the whole shooting match over to the programmers to implement the solution? There are two very good reasons why we do no such thing.

The first reason requires us to remember a fact that was presented early in the book when we first encountered the Software Life Cycle. We pointed out at that time that the maintenance phase of the cycle accounted on average for about 70 per cent of the total life cycle costs. As maintenance costs are closely tied to the time taken by a maintenance programme to comprehend the internal logic of the modules, we should try and aid this process of comprehension.

In Sec. 8.6 we encountered a design heuristic for refining structure that had the same purpose of facilitating programmer comprehension. The heuristic related to module size and the actual statement was — 'a module should contain between 10 and 100 statements'.

But we were also more specific. We referred to some research that showed that a programmer's comprehension dropped rapidly once 30 statements was exceeded.

Quite apart from the question of size, it has been established that the logic of a procedure is more easily and quickly understood if a special detailed design notation has been employed for its display. Thus once again, in the terminology of previous chapters, we place a relatively high weighting on maintainability at the expense of economy.

But why is economy adversely affected if a special detailed design notation is used? The economics referred to here are the economics of software development. Detailed design involves interposing an extra stage between initial design and implementation so that time and expenditure on resources are increased. But on the whole this is acceptable in view of the benefits to be gained during the maintenance phase.

To be fair, the above view is not held universally. A recent paper made a case for coding directly into the programming language Ada, which is an important language that has its antecedents in Pascal. Obviously, such a move only makes sense if Ada is the chosen implementation language. The arguments were very persuasive but we are not convinced. Another reason relates to the idea of software re-usability. This is based on the quite sound argument that there is no point in developing new software if there are modules that can do the required job already in existence. However, life does not stand still, particularly in the volatile world of computing, and fashions in programming languages change quickly. It may well be that when an organization comes to re-use some modules within a new system that it is to be implemented in Fortran 77, say, it finds that they were originally written in an obscure dialect of Slime 43 Autocode. Thus, re-implementation will be necessary, and this is most conveniently achieved if the design is expressed in a stable, language-independent, specialist notation.

As is our usual practice, we propose to offer a modest selection of notations. Two to be precise. But before setting out the stall there is one point to be made. At the initial design stage we took a top-down approach. Prior to that we did the same when analysing and specifying. Even earlier you probably got into the step-wise refinement habit when you developed your first programs. We do not propose to change now and so you will find that the general philosophy of detailed design will be quite familiar.

9.2 DETAILED DESIGN NOTATIONS

A few years ago computer people automatically turned to flowcharting when a detailed design notation was needed. Flowcharting is a highly standardized graphical notation constrained by organizational, national and international conventions. This has the advantage that any designer's flowchart is almost immediately interpretable by any other designer or programmer. Nevertheless, in the light of modern programming language development, flowcharting is now regarded as having a serious defect. This will receive more attention when we come to consider the second of the detailed design notations.

When we considered analysis and specification we introduced a useful notation based on natural language. It was named structured English and it was one of the possible techniques for preparing mini-specs.

A matter for conjecture, therefore, is whether or not the same or similar notation will prove to be satisfactory for expressing the detailed logic of program modules. We hope to show that it can be so. Consequently, we shall examine two notations: one that is natural-language based and another that extends the graphical flowcharting tradition.

9.2.1 Natural language notation

The natural language notation that we shall use is known as *Program Design Language* or *PDL*. Sometimes you will see the term *pseudocode* used for what is a similar concept. You will recall that when we introduced structured English we referred to a quotation that described it as 'a pidgin language that uses the vocabulary of one languague . . . and the syntax of another . . .' The two languages are English and a structured programming language, respectively. The same comment applies to PDL and the quotation was first made in the context of this concept. But there is a difference.

Mini-specs written in structured English have a dual audience, user personnel and computer professionals. For this reason, the rules for their construction may be relaxed if, by so doing, communication is improved. The design of modules needs to be conveyed only to programmers and other designers. Consequently, it is possible and highly desirable that PDL should be applied with greater rigour for it is only by this means that ambiguity may be avoided. This is not to say that no users are interested in the detailed design. Some are, but they appreciate that they must come to terms with the greater formality involved.

Quite apart from change in the level of formality there are two other reasons why mini-specs may not be regarded as equivalent to module designs. For a start, there is not necessarily a one-to-one correspondence between transforms and modules. The process of factoring that the DFDs are subjected to during initial design ensures that this must be so. And many features, the inclusion of which is imperative at the design stage, may well have been ignored during specification. We have in mind the *negative* aspects of a system, e.g., the procedures for dealing with errors, end-of-file situations, and so on. Let us now consider how we should use PDL to express the common design constructs that we shall encounter.

Sequence We should like you to suppose that we are faced with the task of creating the detailed design of a module which is to perform the input, processing and output of a series of numbers. The processing consists of finding the sum of the numbers. The output consists of printing this sum. Our first attempt at design, expressed in PDL, may be as follows:

1 input a series of numbers
2 find the sum of the numbers
3 print the sum

The design has been decomposed into three steps, each of them being at a fairly abstract level. For instance, there is no indication as to how input is to be achieved or how many numbers there are. Each step has been numbered, a feature that was regarded as optional when we used structured English, but which assumes greater significance here. We may say that the three steps represent the top-level design for the module. The design may be decomposed further so that it becomes less abstract. For example, we may know that the user of the module is to be requested to supply a value for n, the number of numbers to be input. We can therefore refine step 1, which becomes

1.1 ask the user for a value for n
1.2 input n
1.3 input a series of n numbers

and the full design is expressed as

1.1 ask the user for a value for n
1.2 input n
1.3 input a series of n numbers
2   find the sum of the numbers
3   print the sum

The process can be continued. Not only may steps 2 and 3 be refined in this manner but any sub-step itself may be subjected to further decomposition. So that we could end up with a set of PDL statements some of which might be labelled 2.1, 2.2.1, 2.2.2, 3.1, etc.

Let us consider another example. A module initializes the first n locations of an array to zero. The procedure obtains the value of n by asking a user to input the value. A possible top-level design for the module could then be produced consisting of three steps as in the previous example:

1   ask the user for the value of n
2   obtain the value of n
3   initialize the first n locations of the array to zero

These steps could then be refined into further sub-steps.

Decision and selection One of the most frequently encountered constructs is the decision procedure with two outcomes. The PDL convention requires that the condition to be tested is delimited by the keywords IF and THEN. The condition is followed by the actions to be performed when the condition holds. Then follows the keyword ELSE and the actions if the condition does not hold. The whole construct is terminated by the keyword END_IF. An example follows:

1   IF the data is valid THEN
2   process the data
3   ELSE
4   perform error routine
5   END_IF

Note that in order to improve the clarity of the presentation we have used indentation. Note also that, in common with the programmer's use of this construct, the ELSE part is not necessarily present.

If in the previous procedure *process the data* consists of adding overtime hours to normal hours, multiplying the total by hourly rate and calculating Schedule E tax, and if *perform error routine* entails printing an error message and incrementing a transaction error count by one, a more refined design for the module may be constructed.

Clearly, the requirement is to decompose the PDL statements 2 and 4, as follows:

```
1    IF the data is valid THEN
2.1      add overtime hours to normal hours
2.2      multiply total hours by hourly rate
2.3      calculate Schedule E tax
3    ELSE
4.1      print error message
4.2      add 1 to transaction error count
5    END__IF
```

Whereas, the IF construct will deal with binary decisions, where a larger number of outcomes are possible then recourse is made to the CASE construct. The condition to be tested is enclosed between the keywords CASE and OF. Each action to be taken is preceded by a value which indicates the outcome of the condition. The construct is terminated by the keyword END__CASE. For instance, a module which analyses and processes transactions in accordance with the transaction code might be expressed as follows:

```
1    CASE transaction code OF
2        01: create new master record
3        02: amend master record
4        03: delete master record
5    END__CASE
```

The CASE statement may also be based on the values of alphabetic strings and an example is provided by the following exercise.

Exercise 9.1 A user of a program which interrogates a file of flight records is allowed to type in three commands: PRINT, DELETE and UPDATE. The command PRINT prints the file, the command DELETE removes all the flight records from the file and the UPDATE command updates a flight record. The top-level design is

```
1    obtain a command
2    process the command
```

Refine the design.

The IF and CASE constructs provide all that we shall need in the way of incorporating decisions or selection into our detailed designs.

Repetition In the course of detailed design there is a frequent need to express the fact that a certain action or group of actions is to be performed a number of times. We shall consider three ways in which PDL may be employed for this purpose. The first, the FOR construct, describes the repetition of actions for a *fixed* number of times. It is used when the designer knows in advance the number of times that actions are to be repeated. The general form of the construct is as follows:

> For variable {FROM start} TO finish {IN STEPS OF value} DO
> actions to be repeatedly performed
> END__FOR

The actions to be repeated are executed with the variable starting with the value *start* and finishing with the value *finish*. The variable is incremented in steps of *value*. The parts in braces are not necessarily present. If *FROM start* is omitted, the default value of the variable is assumed to be one. If *IN STEPS OF value* is omitted, then the variable is incremented in steps of one. An example of the use of the *FOR* construct is given below:

> 1   FOR numbervalue FROM 3 to 101 IN STEPS OF 2 DO
> 2   print numbervalue
> 3   END__FOR

The example conveys that the module is required to print all the odd numbers between 3 and 101 inclusive.

Now consider the following example. One thousand items of data are to be input, processed and placed in the array *logarray* starting at index 100. What will the necessary PDL statements be?

In this case the *IN STEPS OF* part of the construct may be omitted. The top-level design for the module is as follows:

> 1   FOR counter FROM 100 to 1099 DO
> 2   input an item of data
> 3   process the item of data
> 4   place the item of data in logarray
> 5   END__FOR

Often, it is found that an action or group of actions is to be repeated, but for an unknown number of times. An example would be a module that is required to read and process a file of records of unknown length, one at a time. The actions to be performed are enclosed between the keywords REPEAT and UNTIL. The condition which must hold for the repetitions to terminate is written after UNTIL. If we pursue our example of the file of unknown length and specify that the last record in the file contains a marker indicating that it is so, then the top-level design may be expressed as follows:

> 1   REPEAT
> 2   read a record
> 3   process the record
> 4   UNTIL the last record has been processed

The important aspect of the REPEAT construct to remember is that the condition test *succeeds* the actions.

Exercise 9.2 A series of numbers are to be input and processed by a module. The processing consists of finding a count of those numbers which are positive and printing it out. Use the *REPEAT* construct to prepare the detailed design for the module and express it in PDL.

Let us reconsider the example of the file of records of unknown length. Suppose that the file in question, rather than having a special marker in the last record, is terminated by a special record which only contains the symbols EOF, signifying end-of-file. A moment's thought indicates that our *REPEAT* construct is of no value to us now.

Why is this so? You will remember that with *REPEAT* the test of the condition succeeds the actions. This means that in the new circumstances that we have specified, an attempt would be made to process the record at the tail of the file containing EOF alone.

It is unlikely that we would want this to happen. So we really need a construct in which the condition test *precedes* the actions. We can achieve this by means of the *WHILE* construct. With this construct an action or group of actions is repeated *WHILE* a condition holds. The condition to be tested is written between the keywords *WHILE* and *DO*. The actions to be performed then follow and the construct is terminated by the keyword *END__WHILE*. The design for our adapted example with the special EOF record now becomes

```
1   WHILE not EOF record DO
2       read a record
3       process the record
4   END__WHILE
```

Exercise 9.3 A series of messages are to be added to a queue. Each message consists of a destination and a text. If a message is for London then a count is incremented. Finally, the count is printed out. Using a *WHILE* construct, write down a detailed design expressed in PDL.

At this point we have come to the end of the major detailed design constructs that we need. All that remains is to indicate certain housekeeping requirements.

Specifying modules Since we are concerned with the design of the modules that we identified at the initial design stage, we must be able to incorporate our design constructs within a formal framework. In Sec. 8.2 we noted that a module must be 'bounded by boundary elements' and have an 'aggregate identifier'. We also wish to indicate which parameters are input to or output from the modules and if we are obliged to use global data, undesirable though this might be, we should indicate the fact. Therefore, we shall adopt the convention that the name of the module will follow the keyword MODULE. Parameters will be written inside brackets, separated by commas, and will follow the module name.

If global variables are used, the fact should be indicated by the words USES GLOBAL, followed by the variables' names separated by commas, on the line following the module name. The end of a module will be indicated by the keyword END__MODULE. Thus the following

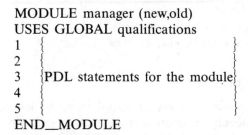

MODULE manager (new,old)
USES GLOBAL qualifications
1 {
2 {
3 {PDL statements for the module}
4 {
5 {
END__MODULE

defines a module named *manager* which has parameters *new* and *old* and uses the global variable *qualifications*.

Module calls One thing that we know for sure is that having gone to the trouble of partitioning our software into modules we must have a mechanism for indicating where these modules are to be called. So a call to another module is indicated by the keyword *CALL* followed by the module's name and the parameters involved. The latter are enclosed in brackets and separated by commas. Thus

CALL keymanager (newkey,validflag)

indicates a call to the module *keymanager* which involves the parameters *newkey* and *validflag*.

When a call to a pre-defined module, such as an operating system routine, is required the word *CALL* is replaced by the keyword *SYSCALL*. So that

SYSCALL createprocess (process__id)

calls the system routine *createprocess* with the parameter *process__id*.

Exercise 9.4 Write a PDL description of a module *patient monitor*. The function of the module is to take a series of 1000 temperature readings from a patient-monitoring system. The module should print out: the average of each 100 readings; the average of all 1000 readings. It should also place in the parameter *difference*, the difference between the average of the 1000 readings and the temperature 98.4. Assume that there is already in existence a module: *getatemp (temp)*.

getatemp places into *temp* the next temperature reading from the monitoring system.

Summary of PDL As you will have gathered, a detailed design written in PDL begins to resemble a set of program statements. But you will have noted also that nothing fancy has been attempted. We have restricted ourselves to the basic constructs and the housekeeping detail necessary to emphasize the individuality of the modules and to enable them to call one another. As we have used the language, conversion into a modern programming language would be straightforward. In fact, translation into something like Cobol or even an assembler language would be no big deal. And that is because we have avoided anything that smacks of language dependence. With justice, it could be said that we have been too pedantic, for we have adhered religiously to the word *module* throughout, whereas many people, particularly those familiar with Pascal or its derivatives, would be happier with *procedure*. But many people would not, and there is no guarantee that procedure will be the OK term a few years hence. So as a good, neutral, non-allusive word, *module* it has to be.

9.2.2 Graphical notation

In Sec. 9.2 we made the point that conventional flowcharts, despite certain advantages, suffer from a serious defect in the context of present-day practice. This defect relates to the nature of modern implementation languages. Whereas Pascal and the like are based on the major constructs of sequence, decision and repetition, conventional flowcharting is not. In fact, flowcharting does not provide a unique symbolism for either of the last two constructs. This means that implementing flowcharts in Pascal, say, is not necessarily a straightforward task, or, to put it another way, flowcharts do not map on to the Pascal language. This will become more clear, we think, when you attempt the exercise that we shall ask you to do a little later.

Accordingly, other graphical notations have been developed in recent years that do provide the requisite mapping and it is one of these that we shall look at now. The notation is known formally as the *design structure diagram*, although for reasons that will become apparent, the term *fall-back diagram* is also used. We shall also use the initials *DSD* for brevity. The notation is described fully in a British Standard Specification (BSI, 1987) but we need only a limited sub-set of the symbols available.

Sequence In Fig. 9.1a we show how a sequence is expressed in accordance with normal flowcharting practice.

Each rectangle, A, B and C represents a block of one or more processing steps. The flow of logical control, as indicated by the small arrows, is vertically downwards and indicates that A is to execute before B, which is to execute before C. The rules which define the sequence in which execution is to take place we shall refer to as *normal rules*.

Contrast this with Fig. 9.1b. We have the same three blocks of processing steps: A, B and C. But now they are joined to a vertical line at N1, N2 and N3. These joins we shall refer to as *nodes*. (It is not normally necessary to label the nodes in this way — we have only done so as an aid to description.) In the description that follows you will encounter the concept of fall-back which is not necessarily easy to grasp. One way of visualizing it is to liken the flow of control to a wave advancing up a beach. It executes (i.e., soaks your hush-puppies and your copy of *Pride and Prejudice*) and falls back (i.e., recedes) before advancing and executing on another path (i.e., drenching another muggins). Once again the flow of control is in accordance with the small arrows. We will follow the course plotted by these arrows and then derive the rules that establish the sequence in which execution is to take place.

(a) Control flows down the main stem.

(b) When it reaches node N1, it takes the left-hand path of the two output paths available to it. (NOTE: It is important to remember that when we write *left-hand path*, this is with respect to the *flow of control* not to the view taken by *you*, the reader.) In taking this path, control meets A and this indicates that A is to execute.

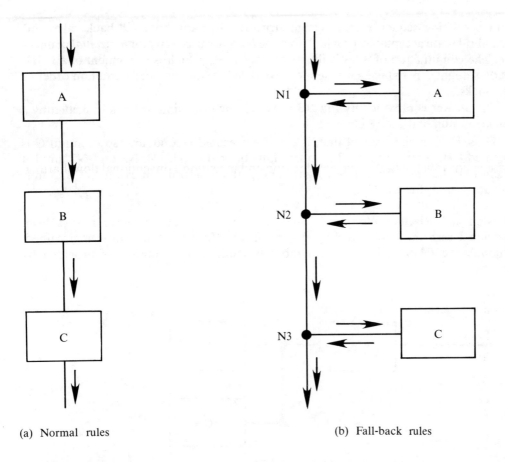

(a) Normal rules   (b) Fall-back rules

Figure 9.1 Flow of control — normal rules and fall-back rules (from BS 6224: 1987).

(c) Control then falls back to N1 where it takes the right-hand path.
(d) It then encounters N2, takes the left-hand path and 'visits' B, thus indicating that B is the next to execute.
(e) Control falls back to N2 and takes the right-hand path to N3.
(f) At N3 the left-hand path is taken, C is visited and thus executes.
(g) Finally, control falls back to N3, takes the right-hand path and proceeds on its way.

The result is that A, B and C maintain the same order of execution as in Fig. 9.1a. But this has been specified by following *fall-back rules*, and these may be summarized as follows:

- Each node consists of *one input path* and *two output paths*.
- At a node, logical control always takes the *left-hand output path*.
- Control always falls back to the nearest node *with an untravelled right-hand path*.
- No executive action takes place during fall-back.

In specifying sequence in a design structure diagram, both fall-back rules and normal rules are acceptable, provided that the *latter* are used only for *horizontal* connection. The combination of rules is illustrated in Fig. 9.2 which is a fragment of a DSD. Readers might care to take a moment or two to deduce the intended execution order of the blocks.

The answer is provided by Fig. 9.3 in which the execution order is indicated by a bracketed numeral alongside each block label.

Thus, D is to be executed first, B is to be executed second, and so on, until C is executed last. Note that after F, control falls back through N4, N3 and N2, until it reaches N1, before it finds a new right-hand path along which it can travel, and thus activate A and, finally, C.

Decision and selection With traditional flowcharting, decisions have always been associated with the diamond-shaped symbol. In DSDs the tradition is maintained, although the relative size of the symbol is reduced. An example is provided by Fig. 9.4.

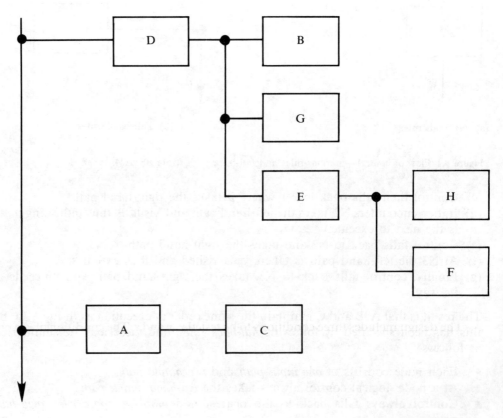

Figure 9.2 Design structure diagram expressing a sequence of processing blocks (adapted from BS 6224: 1987).

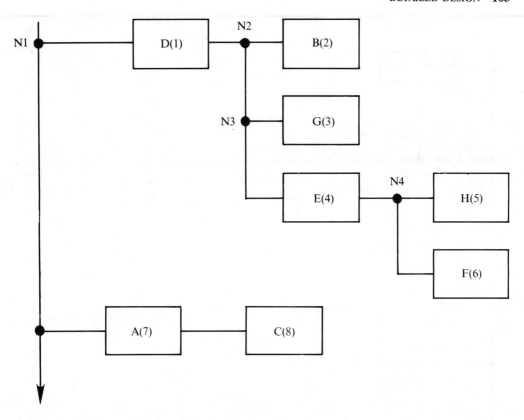

Figure 9.3 Design structure diagram with the order of execution of processing blocks indicated (adapted from BS 6224: 1987).

Figure 9.4a shows the DSD equivalent of the *IF* construct that we met earlier. The condition to be tested is stated in a rectangular box and the alternative paths emanate from the small diamond symbol underneath. After execution of either the *THEN* or *ELSE* branch, control falls back to the node, N. The orientation is fixed and no transposition of the *THEN* and *ELSE* elements is allowed. Figure 9.4b shows the restricted version which omits the *ELSE* elements.

Figure 9.5 represents part of a DSD. What possible sequences of actions could result from this detailed design?

The design includes three conditions to be tested x, y and z. The condition of y is part of a conventional *IF-THEN-ELSE* construct. The others, x and z, have no *ELSE*. The only aspect of the representation that might cause some difficulty is the block A. This alone of the constructs implies the use of normal rules, but you will remember that this is legal. Block A differs from the other elements only in having separate input and output paths for control. So we must visualize control as sweeping *through* block A and falling back by the same route. There are eight possible paths through the design. The alternative sequences are:

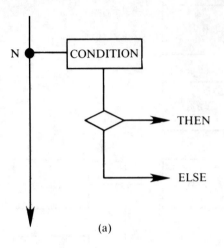

(a)

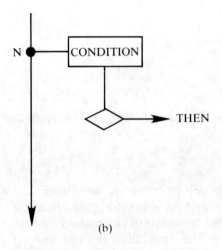

(b)

Figure 9.4 Decisions expressed as DSDs (from BS 6224: 1987).

A, B, C and E
A, B and C
A, B, D and E
A, B, D
A, C and E
A and C
A, D and E
A and D

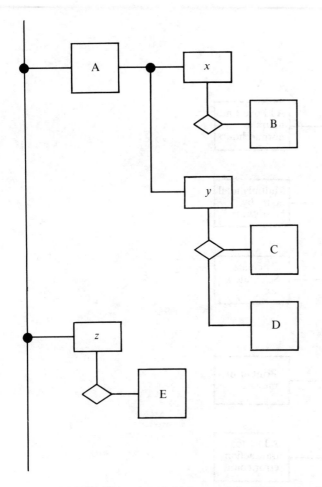

Figure 9.5 DSD illustrating multiple use of the IF construct (from BS 6224: 1987).

In an earlier example we produced the following detailed design:

1   IF the data is valid THEN
2.1   add overtime hours to normal hours
2.2   multiply total hours by hourly rate
2.3   calculate Schedule E tax
3   ELSE
4.1   print error message
4.2   add 1 to transaction error count
5   END_IF

We can express this detailed design as a DSD, Fig. 9.6.

The expression of the *CASE* construct is a logical development of the *IF* symbolism and the general format is shown in Fig. 9.7.

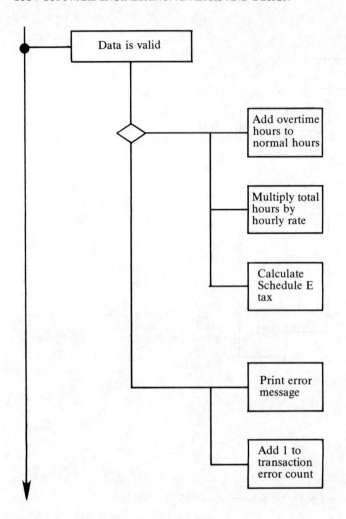

Figure 9.6 A DSD solution to the decision and selection example.

The name of the *CASE* variable is placed in a rectangular box and this leads down to a series of the familiar mini-diamond symbols, one for each significant condition. Each condition is labelled on the left of the corresponding diamond and the appropriate actions are recorded on the right. Thus, condition 1 leads to action A, and so on. Note that proper use of the construct enforces the specification of the actions to be taken if none of the conditions is met. This is achieved by means of a terminal path labelled *ELSE*. This is no bad thing as it ensures that all contingencies are thought through by the designer. After execution of whichever condition branch, control falls back to the node, N.

The solution to Exercise 9.1 can be expressed as a DSD as in Fig. 9.8.

Note how we are forced to consider what should happen if an illegal command such as *AMEND* is entered by the user. Of course, we do not know and, in real life, we would

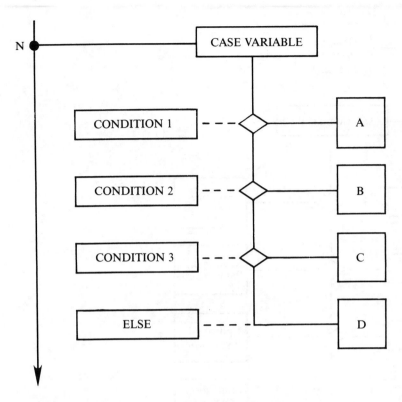

Figure 9.7 Format of the CASE construct (from BS 6224: 1987).

have to find out. For the purpose of this exercise we can assume that the system would rap the user gently on the knuckles with a message such as *illegal command — re-enter*.

Repetition With the expression of repetition constructs, design structure diagram notation breaks completely new ground. The three different varieties of repetition that we discussed earlier are all handled by the use of one new major loop symbol. The general form of the symbol is shown in Fig. 9.9.

The loop control condition is stated in the usual rectangular box. An elongated U-shape represents the clock-wise flow of control around the loop. Any constructs within the loop are joined at nodes on the right-hand side of the U-shape. When repetition terminates, control falls back to node, N. We can commence our examination of the use of the repetition graphic by considering the FOR construct. Earlier we produced the following detailed design:

```
1  FOR counter FROM 100 to 1099 DO
2      input an item of data
3      process the item of data
4      place the item of data in logarray
5  END_FOR
```

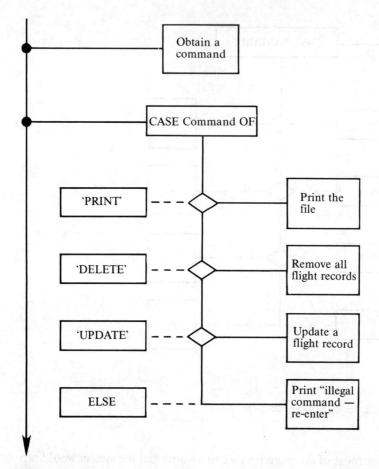

Figure 9.8 A DSD solution to Exercise 9.1.

This design expressed in DSD notation would be as shown in Fig. 9.10.

The loop control condition box contains much the same wording as line 1 of the PDL solution and the actions to be executed repeatedly are hung from nodes on the right-hand side. In general, the diagram for repetition as shown in Fig. 9.9 implies that the loop condition is evaluated at the head of the loop, e.g., before A in Fig. 9.9. Where the implementation language allows specification of the evaluation point, the notations of Fig. 9.11 may be employed.

In each of the three cases shown, the evaluation point is indicated by a pair of short parallel lines intersecting the flow of the loop. This raises a mildly controversial point. The use of this feature begins to make the notation a little implementation-language dependent. If we take mid-point evaluation as an example, we know that Pascal does

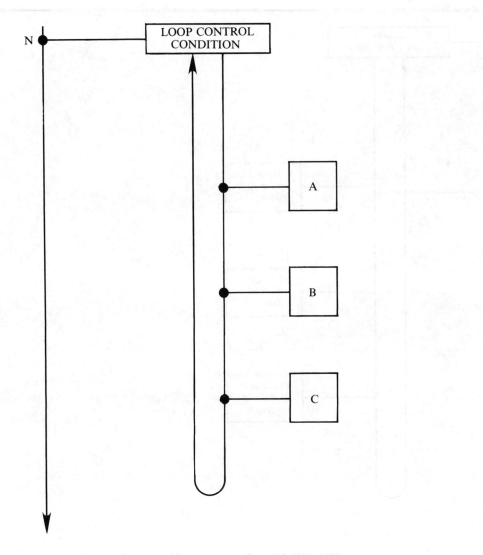

Figure 9.9 Format of the repetition construct (from BS 6224: 1987).

not allow this. But some programming languages, e.g., the language C, do. This means that if the software is to be implemented in Pascal, the programmers would not thank the designer for designing-in mid-point evaluation. Whereas, if C is the chosen vehicle, the situation would pass without comment. So that the whole argument for employing a special detailed-design notation becomes muddied. To retain the purity of the detailed design concept it is best to avoid such features if at all possible. In using the repetition graphic there is a stylistic point that should be observed. The looped line should be extended downwards at least as far as the lowest construct contained within the loop. This is a considerable aid to clarity. We will now look at two more examples.

The detailed design for Exercise 9.3 is expressed as a DSD in Fig. 9.12.

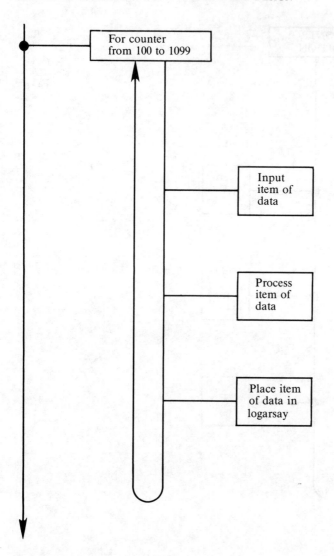

Figure 9.10 A DSD for a FOR loop.

For the sake of clarity we have numbered the symbols so that you may match them with the original PDL statements. You will note that there are no symbolic equivalents to 2.5 END_IF and 2.7 END_WHILE as these are not necessary with the graphical notation that we are employing. Note finally that we have not shown explicitly where the loop condition is to be tested. This is because, in default of actually specifying the point of evaluation, the head of the loop is assumed. And this is where we want it to be.

Now look at the detailed design for Exercise 9.2 expressed as a DSD, Fig. 9.13.

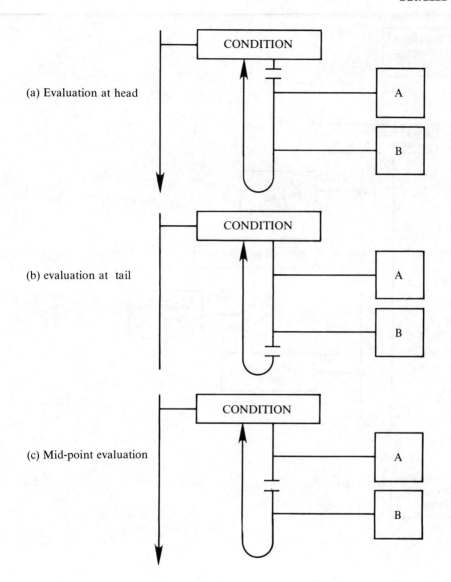

Figure 9.11 Repetition with specification of evaluation point (from BS 6224: 1987).

The only feature to note here is that we are now dealing with the *REPEAT* construct so that we are interested in evaluating the loop condition after the repeated activities have been executed. Consequently, we show the evaluation symbol of two parallel lines at the tail of the loop.

Designators, annotation and module calls As with PDL a moderate amount of tidying up is necessary to make a detailed design expressed in DSD into a complete entity. This is

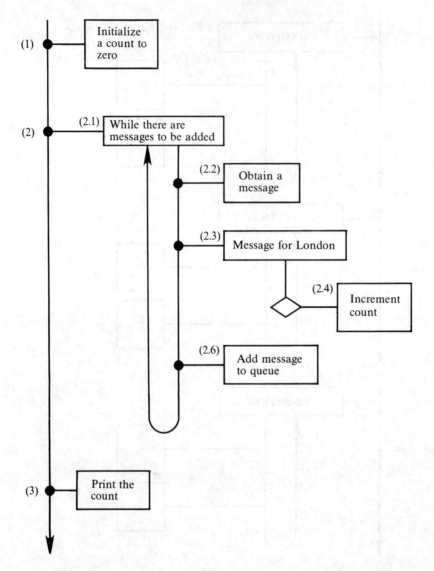

Figure 9.12 A DSD answer to Exercise 9.3.

achieved largely by means of one further symbol, the designator. The symbol used is identical to the very familiar terminator symbol from conventional flowcharts, i.e., it is a rectangle with rounded ends. However, it is put to more varied use. On occasion it is necessary to revert to natural language, by way of explanatory notes, in order to convey the maximum of information to others. This is achieved by means of the following symbol:

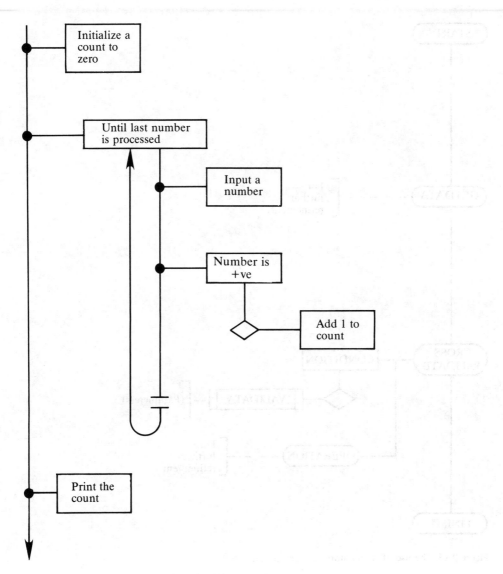

Figure 9.13 A DSD answer to Exercise 9.2.

⎡ descriptive
⎯ ⎯ ⎯
⎣ text

Some of the uses of designators and annotation are demonstrated in Fig. 9.14.

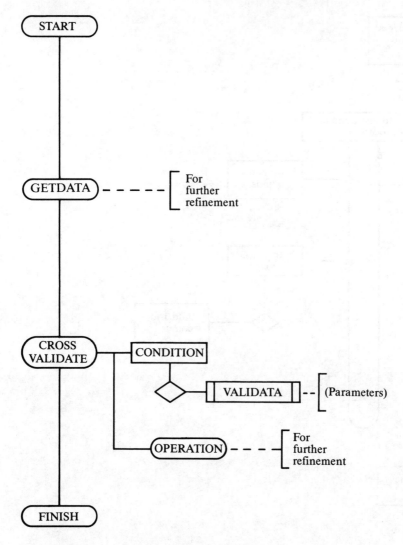

Figure 9.14 The use of designators and annotation.

First, the designator provides the necessary isolating boundary elements at the beginning and end of the module. In Fig. 9.14 these are shown with the words *START* and *FINISH* inside them. Alternatively, they may contain *BEGIN* and *END*. Second, they may be used to section the detailed design into parts. So we could if we wished have a DSD consisting entirely of designators as the top-level design — much as we used statements in PDL labelled with single digit numerals, 1, 2, 3, etc., for the same purpose. If we inspect Fig. 9.14 and look along the vertical line between the start and finish designators, we see the top-level for this particular module. This leads into a third role: to designate sections due for further refinement. In the diagram the designator labelled **GETDATA** indicates that a major section of the module has yet to be defined in detail.

Similarly, OPERATION, which is a sub-section of CROSS VALIDATE, needs to be refined further. Where a module call is to be indicated, a striped rectangle is used. The name of the called module appears within the symbol as is the case with VALIDATA in the diagram. We have used annotation to identify the reasons for using the designator symbol for GETDATA and OPERATION, and also for recording the parameters used in the module call.

Exercise 9.5 Convert the conventional flowchart of Fig. 9.15 into a DSD.

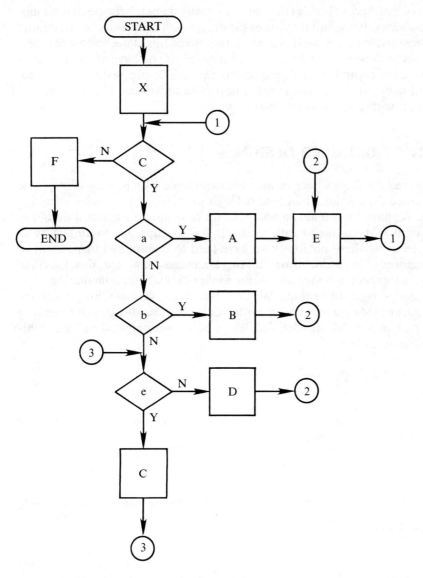

Figure 9.15 Flowchart for conversion into a DSD (Exercise 9.5) (adapted from BS 6224: 1987).

Summary of DSDs Is a 'picture worth a thousand words'? Well, as a colleague of ours has said: 'it depends on the picture and it depends on the words.' As he is in the picture business (he is a computer graphics expert), we take his caution seriously. There is no point in preparing detailed designs in a notation that may frequently require re-formatting before they are of any use. But we do believe that design structure diagrams provide a rational, graphical alternative for those who prefer pictures to text. DSDs are easily produced. A criticism is often made of graphical notations that they are, unless there is a suitable drawing template available, tedious to construct. There are templates for DSDs available, with the correct British Standard symbols, although at the time of writing they are not easily come by. But that does not really matter. Because of their top-to-bottom, left-to-right construction they are easily drawn with mechanical or electronic aids. If you are prepared to abjure such niceties as the curved bits at the bottom of loops, a pretty fair job can be done with a typewriter — better still, if you have access to a half-decent text editor on a computer. A final point is that DSDs are easily maintained. Because of the fall-back rules it is quite easy to insert extra constructs. This, of course, is often quite difficult with conventional flowcharts.

9.3 SUMMARY OF DETAILED DESIGN

We have now reached the stage where we are able to produce, by a process of step-wise refinement, a detailed description of the internal logic of each of the modules identified by initial design. We have looked at two notations for recording the detailed design so that implementation may go ahead with relatively few hiccups due to ambiguity or incompleteness. In using these notations we have tried to remain as independent as possible of the nuances of individual programming languages for we are conscious that, largely speaking, we expect a design to outlive any particular implementation.

There is one design task outstanding. We have not, as yet, said anything about the design of data structures. As we mentioned earlier, data structure design will often take place, at least in part, in parallel with detailed design. So we must now take a look at this aspect of the designer's work.

REFERENCE

BSI (1987) *BS 6224: Guide to Design Structure Diagrams for use in program design and other logic applications*, British Standards Institution, London.

DATA STRUCTURE DESIGN

10.1 INTRODUCTION

So far our design activities have been entirely devoted to programs. Prominent among our design criteria has been the property of maintainability. As we turn our attention to ,the design of data structures we will often find that economy will rival maintainability as our prime criterion. The reason why this is so is that for a very large proportion of computer applications, particularly in real-time and commercial data processing categories, the software *performance*, i.e., the proportion of computing resources used and the time that they are used for, depends almost entirely on the data structures selected. So that operating economy is dependent on the chosen structures also. On the other hand, it should be borne in mind that efforts to maximize performance via data structure design may result in software that is complex and difficult to maintain. So we encounter a classical trade off situation, economy against maintainability.

Before tackling data design proper, it is necessary to remind ourselves of its purpose. Data has no intrinsic value. What value it has lies entirely in its ability to say something about the real world. For instance, the shareholder of an enterprise scanning the most recent balance sheet will find it to be of value only to the extent that it has something to say about the company concerned. Similarly, we would expect a radar operator to be less interested in an unexpected blip on the screen than in the object that it might represent. We might, in fact, draw an analogy between data and the real world on one hand, and a five pound note and wealth on the other. The five pound note has no intrinsic value either but it indicates that the real-world owner is worth at least that much.

In the real world, data has a dual role. It has something to say about *things* (*entities* is the OK word), and the *relationships* between things of different types. Just note that *entity types* can cover a wide range, for they may encompass people, tasks, objects, both natural and artificial, events such as the arrival of messages, and so on.

It is usual at this point to ask you to consider the various entity types that exist around you in a college or university. We will not be unusual. No doubt you will be happy, with *student* as an entity type. You may also consider some of *course, tutor, lecturer, professor*, and so on. If we caught you in a moment of morbid introspection then you may have included *assignment, course fee* and *examination*.

If analysis and specification has taken the route that we charted earlier in the book, then we shall have a description of the data that is used in the application area of interest. It will be in the data dictionary which has been defined as 'a repository of data about data' (Martin, 1976). However, data as we meet it in the real world is far removed from the patterns of bits that will represent it in computer storage. We say that real-world data is *abstract data* whereas the corresponding bit patterns are *concrete data*. So we are now in the position where we can define what *data structure design* is all about. It is concerned with reducing the degree of abstraction in such a way that its representation within the computing machinery enables effective and efficient processing. To be absolutely fair, this is not achieved by the designer unaided. He or she will receive some help along the way. The nature of this help will become apparent in Sec. 10.3, as will the concept of different levels of abstraction.

10.2 REVIEW OF SIMPLE DATA STRUCTURES

It is advisable at this point to review briefly some of the simple data structures that you will have encountered already. The key structures with their definitions are as follows:

- *array* — A one-dimensional array is a data structure in which, corresponding to each integer from a pre-defined fixed range, there is an item of information of a pre-defined type. The concept can be generalized to that of an N-dimensional array, in which each element of a pre-defined type is uniquely identified by a set of N integers from a set of N pre-defined fixed ranges.
- *record* — A data structure which contains several fields, in a pre-defined fixed order, where each field has a distinct identifier and contains an item of information of a pre-defined type.
- *sequence* — A structure in which zero or more items of information of a pre-defined type are placed one after another in an order determined by some pre-defined relationship.
- *tree* — A data structure which has zero or more nodes organized in a hierarchical manner such that: (a) except when the tree is empty, there is one node called the root, at the highest level; (b) every node, except the root, is joined by a branch to just one node at the next higher level; (c) one item of information of a pre-defined type is associated with each node; (d) a pre-defined relationship exists between the information on adjacent levels.

We should recall also that the four structures defined above may be divided into two categories in accordance with one important property. The two categories are *static* data structures and *dynamic* data structures.

If a data structure is static then its structure will always remain the same, although the data stored in that structure may be changed. If a data structure is dynamic then both the structure and the data may change. Consequently, arrays and records come into the static category. Sequences and trees are dynamic. Finally, we should remember the existence of *composite data structures*, i.e., data structures, the components of which are themselves simple data structures.

10.3 MODELLING THE REAL WORLD

Let us imagine that somewhere in the real world there is a builder who employs three bricklayers, Kevin, Leroy and Paddy. His three employees are paid weekly on the basis of the number of hours that they work on each of the weekdays, Monday to Friday. The builder needs to keep a record of the daily hours worked so that he can pay them at the end of the week. Let us assume that a convenient recording method for him is to keep notes in his diary. If we inspect a typical page of his diary, we might see something resembling Fig. 10.1.

The diary makes riveting reading. But we must put aside any conjectures as to the identity of the mysterious J. with whom the builder is due to lunch at the 'Spotted Dog' on Wednesday, and concentrate on the content that is relevant to the task in hand. This involves actually paying Leroy, Paddy and Kev for the work that they have done. In this context, the content that is significant is highlighted on the diagram. It can be seen that this significant data may be regarded as a number of *pairs* of data items, each one having the format *<name, hours>*, although through lack of time or the exigencies of space our builder has resorted to various formats and abbreviations in compiling his record. Look at the significant data item pairs for Friday 23 September. The builder has written 'All 7 hours'. This, presumably, means that all three brickies worked for seven hours on that day, so that the relevant pairs are: *Kevin 7 Leroy 7 Paddy 7*.

It is quite ridiculous to contemplate using the diary page as it stands as the basis for the weekly payroll. It is more sensible to extract the necessary information and format it appropriately for subsequent processing. This extraction process is known as *conceptual modelling*.

10.3.1 Conceptual modelling

A conceptual model of data is a representation that not only shows that data, but also preserves the relationships between the different data items. Further, the conceptual model should exclude all that is irrelevant to the task in hand. Except for the most trivial circumstances, a number of conceptual models are usually derivable in a given real-world situation. For example, in the case of the bricklayers' payroll, we might regard a *sequence* as providing a suitable conceptual model. Such a sequence is shown in Fig. 10.2.

Note that we have chosen to preserve the relationship between each bricklayer's hours worked and the day of the week on which they took place, so that the sequence is a sequence of *triples*, simple *records* consisting of three data items, with the format *<day_name_hours>*.

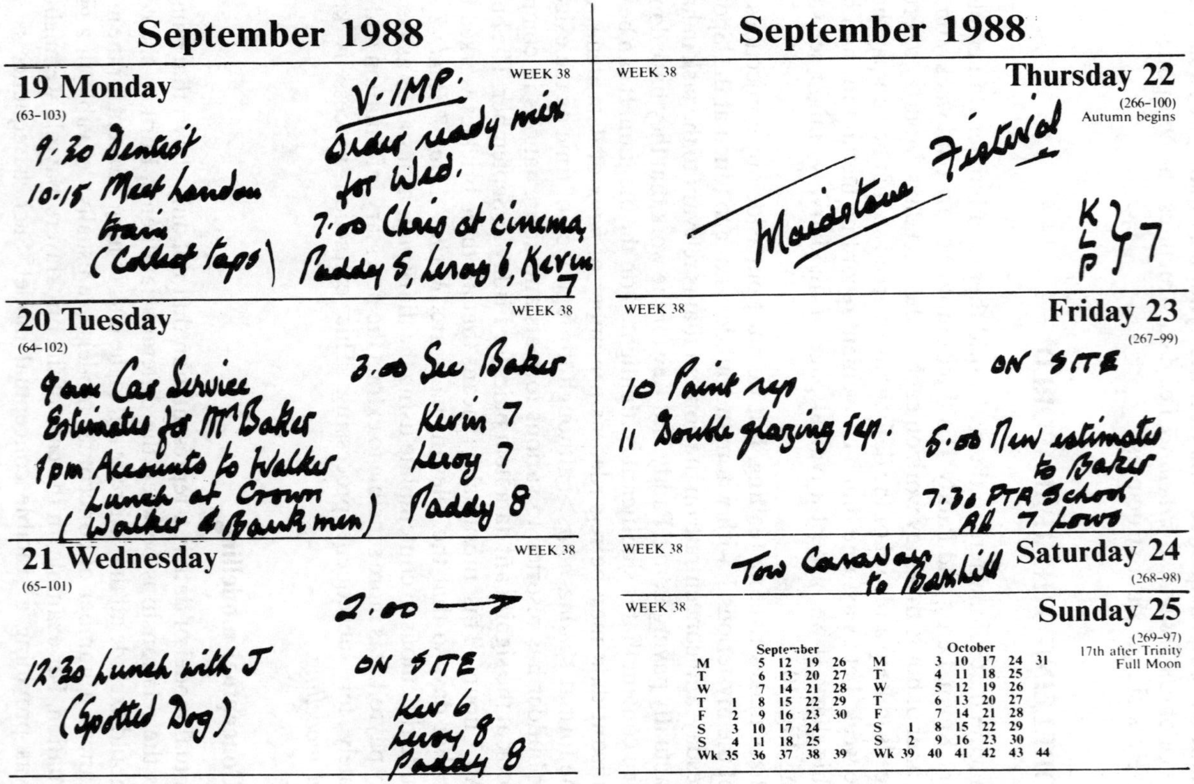

September 1988

September 1988

19 Monday
(63–103)   WEEK 38

V. IMP.
Order ready mix
for Weds
10·15 Meet London
train
7.00 Chris at cinema
(Collect tapes) (Paddy 5, Long 6, Kevin 7)

20 Tuesday
(64–102)   WEEK 38

9am Car Service
Estimates for Mr Baker
1pm Accounts to Walker
Lunch at Corner
(Walker & Bankman)   3.00 See Baker
                                  Kevin 7
                                  Long 7
                                  Paddy 8

21 Wednesday
(65–101)   WEEK 38

12.30 lunch with J
(Spotted Dog)
                                  2.00 →
                                  ON SITE
                                  Kev 6
                                  Long 7
                                  Paddy 8

Thursday 22
(266–100)
Autumn begins   WEEK 38

Manchester Zealand

K ½ 7
P ꞌ 7

Friday 23
(267–99)

ON SITE

10 Paint 149
11 Banks glazing 149.
6.00 New estimate
to Baker
7.30 PTA School
At 7 Lanes

Saturday 24
(268–98)   WEEK 38

Two Canalways
to Bramhill →

ON SITE

Sunday 25
(269–97)
17th after Trinity
Full Moon

September						October						
M	5	12	19	26		M	3	10	17	24	31	
T	6	13	20	27		T	4	11	18	25		
W	7	14	21	28		W	5	12	19	26		
T	1	8	15	22	29	T	6	13	20	27		
F	2	9	16	23	30	F	7	14	21	28		
S	3	10	17	24		S	1	8	15	22	29	
S	4	11	18	25		S	2	9	16	23	30	
Wk	35	36	37	38	39	Wk	39	40	41	42	43	44

Figure 10.1 A page from the builder's diary.

122

Monday	Kevin	7
Monday	Leroy	6
Monday	Paddy	5
Tuesday	Kevin	7
Tuesday	Leroy	7
Tuesday	Paddy	8
Wednesday	Kevin	6
Wednesday	Leroy	8
Wednesday	Paddy	8
Thursday	Kevin	7
Thursday	Leroy	7
Thursday	Paddy	7
Friday	Kevin	7
Friday	Leroy	7
Friday	Paddy	7

Figure 10.2 A conceptual model for the builder's payroll data (1).

Looking at the sequence in Fig. 10.2 it can be seen it is ordered and that the triples are, first of all, grouped by *day*. Within each group, they are ordered by *name*. We could say that they are ordered on *day/name* or, alternatively, that they are ordered by *name within day*.

This sequence provides quite a good conceptual model if the builder is interested in the relationship between *hours* and *days*. This may be the case if he wishes to accumulate the costs of a project day by day. But the avowed object of the exercise is to pay the brickies and this particular conceptual model is not ideal for this purpose.

This is because the records for each individual are separated in the sequence, so that the aggregated weekly hours per employee are not immediately apparent. Perhaps you can do better as, by now, you should be able to suggest another conceptual model, based on sequence, that would be preferred.

A possibility is to order the sequence of triples by *day within name*, in which case it would appear as in Fig. 10.3.

Monday	Kevin	7
Tuesday	Kevin	7
Wednesday	Kevin	6
Thursday	Kevin	7
Friday	Kevin	7
Monday	Leroy	6
Tuesday	Leroy	7
Wednesday	Leroy	8
Thursday	Leroy	7
Friday	Leroy	7
Monday	Paddy	5
Tuesday	Paddy	8
Wednesday	Paddy	8
Thursday	Paddy	7
Friday	Paddy	7

Figure 10.3 A conceptual model for the builder's payroll data (2).

The total hours worked are now available at a glance (plus a little mental arithmetic) and we might claim, with some justification, that we now have an improved conceptual model. But, let us suppose that the builder is equally interested in maintaining a daily project cost summary *and* paying his employees. Under these circumstances yet another conceptual model might suggest itself. This model is illustrated in Fig. 10.4.

	Monday	*Tuesday*	*Wednesday*	*Thursday*	*Friday*
Kevin	7	7	6	7	7
Leroy	6	7	8	7	7
Paddy	5	8	8	7	7

Figure 10.4 A conceptual model for the builder's payroll and project data.

We now have what is best described as a *table* or, if you wish, a one-dimensional *array of records*. Both types of summary data, by employee and by day, are easily derived.

Total hours worked for each employee may be obtained by summing the rows of the table. Total hours worked for each day is derived by summing the columns.

Let us assume that we decide that the tabular representation provides the best conceptual model for the builder's purpose. What we have done is to consider three models (two different sequences and a table), and select one (the table). So we have done some design. But there is something else to note. The three models are, of course, examples of data structures. But as they have been formulated purely on their ability to represent real-world data in a useful and efficient way, and take no account of computer software or hardware, we refer to them as abstract data structures. So what we have really done is to design an abstract data structure for the application. We are still some way from bit patterns so let us examine the remainder of the modelling process.

10.3.2 Logical modelling

It is all well and good for us to decide on a table as being the preferred abstract data structure, but as our decision was arrived at from a real-world point of view, there is no guarantee that the programming language that will be used to implement the structure can actually handle tables. Thus, the process of *logical modelling* entails converting our chosen abstract structure into a concrete data structure, i.e., one that the implementation language can handle. Of course, if the implementation language *can* handle tables, then the abstract and the concrete structures are the same. Returning to the builder's payroll application, let us consider the implication of knowing that the implementation language that will be used can only handle one type of data structure, the *array*. *Logical modelling* now hinges on the question as to whether or not our chosen abstract data structure, the table, can be converted to the concrete data structure, the array. It can, of course, and we would represent the logical model as a two-dimensional array, *H*, as in Fig. 10.5.

$$H = \begin{pmatrix} 7 & 7 & 6 & 7 & 7 \\ 6 & 7 & 8 & 7 & 7 \\ 5 & 8 & 8 & 7 & 7 \end{pmatrix}$$

Figure 10.5 A logical model for the builder's payroll and project data.

We merely omit the row and column headings and enclose the hour data in brackets in order to represent the concrete data structure. In this case there was no choice available in determining what the concrete data structure should be. But it is easy to imagine that if the abstract data structure had been more complex and if the implementation language had been more flexible in terms of its data structure handling capability, then a real choice might have been available. So we conclude that frequently an element of design enters the logical modelling process. Design requires criteria and the criteria used in logical modelling usually relate to performance.

Now consider a small change in the scenario. When business is good our long suffering builder sometimes employs (in addition to Kevin, Leroy and Paddy) Kevin's brother Gary, Leroy's cousin Adrian and two Australians, Neil and Bruce, who are trying to save enough money to tour Europe. Can we build a conceptual model of the real-world data?

Clearly we now have a number of elements that can vary from week to week. The workload may not justify employing more than the three regulars, Gary may decide to go back to foreign exchange dealing, or Neil and Bruce may decide that they have saved enough to get to Calais anyway, and disappear. So it would seem that a dynamic structure such as a sequence, the elements of which are records, might be suitable. Such a sequence is shown in Fig. 10.6.

We see that we have an abstract data structure that is similar to Fig. 10.4. The major difference is that whereas Fig. 10.4 is a table of fixed length, Fig. 10.6 is of varying length, week by week. This must be so in order that we can take into account the volatile nature of the builder's workforce.

We can develop two logical models from the above conceptual model on the basis that the implementation language can handle arrays and records. Two possible means of implementing the sequence are shown in Fig. 10.7.

Basically, the diagram shows a contiguous representation (a), and an instance of a linked representation (b), of the sequence. In each case the concrete data structure is a one-dimensional array of records and has certain integer variables associated with it. The records in (b) are longer than in (a) as they incorporate a link field. In each case also, the size of the array has been chosen to be large enough to hold the maximum number of records likely to occur in the sequence. Assuming that you have a knowledge of the data structures available in Pascal you should be able to work out how the basic operations of access, record insertion and record deletion take place.

Exercise 10.1 What trade off in terms of performance would you expect to be considered in selecting one of the two logical models?

Thus, in real life, the decision would depend on the availability of memory space

Name	Monday	Tuesday	Wednesday	Thursday	Friday
Adrian	0	0	0	8	7
Bruce	7	6	0	0	0
Gary	7	6	5	0	0
Kevin	7	8	9	9	9
Leroy	7	8	9	8	9
Neil	7	6	0	0	0
Paddy	7	8	6	7	6

Figure 10.6 A conceptual model for the builder's data with a varying workforce.

and the frequency of occurrence of additions to and deletions from the sequence. Although we still have not reached the stage of bits in the machine, we are nearly at the end of the road. There is one final stage of modelling to be considered.

10.3.3 Physical modelling

This part of the process is concerned with where we store the data in the computer's memory. Let us return to the original logical model for the builder's payroll and project data, Fig. 10.5. The data in array H, come execution time, will occupy certain elements of computer storage. Here all the decisions have already been taken, by the designer of the operating software, so that we have no physical modelling to do. The physical model may be as shown in Fig. 10.8, the data occupying contiguous elements of primary storage in the address range 2453 to 2467 inclusive. We could refer to Fig. 10.8 as a memory map.

			Name	Monday	Tuesday	Wednesday	Thursday	Friday
Size	7	0						
		1	Adrian	0	0	0	8	7
		2	Bruce	7	6	0	0	0
		3	Gary	7	6	5	0	0
Limit	20	4	Kevin	7	8	9	9	9
		5	Leroy	7	8	9	8	9
		6	Neil	7	6	0	0	0
		7	Paddy	7	8	6	7	6
		•						
		•						
		•						
		20						

(a)

		Name	M	Tu	W	Th	F	Link
Limit	20	1 Paddy	7	8	6	7	6	3
		2 Leroy	7	8	9	8	9	8
S	3	3			DUMMY RECORD			7
		4 Gary	7	6	5	0	0	6
Free	5	5						9
		6 Kevin	7	8	9	9	9	2
		7 Adrian	0	0	0	8	7	10
		8 Neil	7	6	0	0	0	7
		9						11
		10 Bruce	7	6	0	0	0	4
		•						
		•						
		•						
		20						

(b)

Figure 10.7 Two logical models for the builder's data with a varying workforce.

Physical address of primary storage location	Value
2453	7
2454	7
2455	6
2456	7
2457	7
2458	6
2459	7
2460	8
2461	7
2462	7
2463	5
2464	8
2465	8
2466	7
2467	7

Figure 10.8 A physical model for the builder's payroll and project data.

10.3.4 Summary

We can summarize the stages of modelling the real world in a graphic manner, as in Fig. 10.9.

As we are in the business of software design, in the application rather than the operating or support sense, we should carefully consider our role in the sequence of modelling stages that we have just discussed. It is clear, we think, that *physical modelling* is well outside our remit. This is a matter for systems programmers and the designers of the software environment for the target machine on which the new system will be implemented. This leaves us with *conceptual* and *logical modelling* to consider. As there was no doubt in our minds that physical modelling is no concern of the applications software designer, equally there is no doubt that conceptual modelling is very much his or her concern. The designer working with user specifications is in the best possible

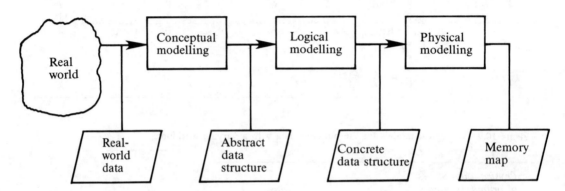

Figure 10.9 The stages of modelling real-world data.

position to develop abstract data structures from real-world situations. We are left with the middle stage of logical modelling. We pointed out that, under certain circumstances, this modelling stage involved elements of design activity.

Let us remind you what these circumstances are: if the abstract data structure is complex and if the implementation language is generously endowed with data structure handling facilities, then choice is involved in logical modelling and this is a design activity.

But remember that throughout our study of software design we have tried to remain aloof from implementation, the reason being that programming languages change fairly rapidly and we want our design to remain valid for a long time. If we are to persevere with this policy we must not get involved in the design of concrete data structures, for these are implementation dependent. This restriction has an important side-effect that the designer must be aware of. Even if the designer knows what the concrete data structure will be, he or she must not allow this to influence the detailed design. For example, if an abstract data structure has been designed as a sequence but it is known that it will be implemented as an array, the designer must not be tempted to assume that the sequence may be indexed by number. For a subsequent change in implementation language may mean that the concrete data structure is no longer an array and the detailed design will be invalidated.

In summary, therefore, we can say that data structure design is the design of abstract data structures. The design of concrete data structures is part of the programmer's job.

You may sense that there is some danger in this separation of roles, and there is. You might wonder what happens if a designer chooses an abstract data structure that is unimplementable. Well, in the vast majority of cases the designer will not. If the design is based on the simple data structures reviewed in Sec. 10.2, or composites based on them, the situation is unlikely to arise. If it does, you have our solemn word that the programmers will waste little time in requesting the designer to think again.

10.4 DESIGN NOTATIONS

There is little in the way of recognized conventions for representing abstract data structures. Most designers tend to use diagrammatic notations of the types with which you will be familiar from your initial exposure to data structure concepts. It is an area in which more formality would, perhaps, be rather welcome. If you have the opportunity to read the guide to the use of design structure diagrams (BSI, 1987), you will see that there is a small section devoted to their use for data structure design. It must be admitted that the use of DSDs in this context is not well developed. However, our personal view is that DSD is a promising data structure design tool and we may see it used more widely in this context in the years to come.

10.5 SUMMARY OF DATA STRUCTURE DESIGN

We have seen that data structure design is essentially the design of abstract data structures. They should be based, if possible, on the simple data structures reviewed in Sec. 10.2 or on composite structures derived from them. The designs are often expressed diagrammatically, although no strict convention applies to this expression. The choice of concrete data structures is implementation dependent and is best left to the programming staff to effect. Thus, the validity of the design is preserved despite any changes in the implementation language.

REFERENCES

BSI (1987) *BS 6224: 1987 Guide to Design Structure Diagrams for use in program design and other logic applications*, British Standards Institution, London.
Martin, J. (1976) *Principles of Data-Base Management*, Prentice-Hall, Englewood Cliffs, New Jersey.

11

DESIGN DOCUMENTATION

11.1 INTRODUCTION

As we have said before, the main means of communication between the designers and the programmers is by means of the design document. We have already devoted a considerable amount of attention to the notations that are suitable for inclusion, but now we must consider the design document as a whole. This is by no means the sole output of the design phase. There are other documents that are most appropriately produced concurrently, at least in their initial or prototype form. These include the systems manual, the user manual and the user guide.

Although various professional bodies, such as the Computer Society of the Institute of Electrical and Electronics Engineers of the USA, have recommended guidelines for their production (IEEE, 1986), there is nothing in the way of an international or national standard for any of these documents. Consequently, most organizations with computer experience will have firm ideas of their own as to content and format.

11.2 THE DESIGN DOCUMENT

The document may masquerade under a number of different names; we shall encounter one of them in a moment. But whatever the name this document must be regarded as the prime product or, if you insist, 'deliverable' emanating from the design phase. It should, in theory, permit a smooth implementation of the software without any hitches. As you will know by now, life is not that simple and there will almost always be snags of one sort or another. Even so, a carefully prepared design document should keep such hiccups to a minimum.

Normally, the notations created by the designers will be embedded within other key material. A typical format is shown in Fig. 11.1. This has been adapted from a book on software engineering (Pressman, 1982).

It should be stated at the outset that this proposed format is comprehensive and it is very likely that for many software projects not every listed item is appropriate.

The first point to note is that Pressman has entitled the document *Software Design Specification*, this being one of the many aliases mentioned hitherto. The title is semantically correct, we suppose, but personally speaking we prefer not to use the word *specification* for a document produced at this stage of the cycle. *Sections 3.0, 4.0* and *5.0* correspond broadly with our three phases of design: initial, detailed and data structure design. Consequently, they will be largely based on the types of notation that we have covered in previous chapters. A point of special interest here is *Section 5.3, File and data cross-reference*. This associates different items of data, records, and so on with the individual modules in which they are used. This clearly should be of inestimable value for the testing and subsequent maintenance of the system.

These sections are preceded by *1.0 Scope* and *2.0 Reference documents*. The first of these describes the context in which the software is being developed and much of the included information relates to earlier stages of the life cycle. In fact, *objectives (1.1)* and *constraints (1.5)* will have appeared on the scene as part of the initial user requirement document. The latter section merely lists the supporting documentation to which reference has been made in arriving at the chosen design. This may include material referring to existing procedures and to the hardware/software environment in which the new software is to function.

Section 6.0 is concerned with testing. Although a detailed testing plan cannot be proposed at this stage, guidelines for the testing and integration of modules should be laid down. The general philosophy towards testing will originate with the user so that the rigour or otherwise of the testing procedures will be application dependent. For example, the project sponsors for defence systems will quite properly insist on very high testing standards. The company maintaining address lists for largely unwanted mailshots will be less concerned with this aspect.

Section 7.0 Packaging is concerned with performance and may originate with preferences expressed in the user requirement document. For instance, if a design objective is to minimize the physical occupation of primary storage then it may be necessary for the implementers to organize or *package* the software in such a way that this objective is achieved.

This version of the design document ends with sections designed to record any special information or appendix material.

We think we can draw a useful analogy at this point. When we considered data structure design we described it as a progression from the abstract to the concrete. Much the same description may be applied to the production of the design document. We start with a series of abstractions in the early days of the cycle and progressively firm up until the relatively concrete design document is available. The point is that we should not expect the designer to finish the design, push it to one side and then proceed to compile the document. The document should *evolve* throughout the design stage so that it is available shortly after the creative work is finished. With the common availability of word processors there is no reason why design documentation should not be produced in this fashion.

Software Design Specification

1.0 Scope
    1.1 System objective and software's role as a system element
    1.2 Hardware, software, and human interfaces
    1.3 Major software functions
    1.4 Externally defined database
    1.5 Major design constraints and limitations

2.0 Reference documents
    2.1 Existing software documentation
    2.2 System documentation
    2.3 Vendor (hardware or software) documents
    2.4 Technical references

3.0 Design description
    3.1 Data description
        3.1.1 Review of information flow
        3.1.2 Review of information structure
    3.2 Derived software structure
    3.3 Interfaces within structure

4.0 Modules
    For each module:
    4.1 Processing narrative
    4.2 Interface description
    4.3 Design language (or other) description
    4.4 Modules used
    4.5 Data organization
    4.6 Comments

5.0 File structure and global data
    5.1 External file structure
        5.1.1 Logical structure
        5.1.2 Logical record description
        5.1.3 Access method
    5.2 Global data
    5.3 File and data cross-reference

6.0 Test provisions
    6.1 Test guidelines
    6.2 Integration strategy
    6.3 Special considerations

7.0 Packaging
    7.1 Special program overlay provisions
    7.2 Transfer considerations

8.0 Special notes

9.0 Appendices

Figure 11.1 A possible format for the design document (adapted from Pressman, 1982).

11.3 OTHER DOCUMENTS

We are now in some difficulty. The other documents that we wish to mention are so dependent on the type of user and the nature of the application that it is almost impossible even to suggest guidelines. We must content ourselves, therefore, with a few remarks that it is hoped will be useful.

11.3.1 Systems manual

The systems manual is intended to be a guide for those who will maintain the software once it is in operation. We should be clear at once that this document will not be complete at the end of the design stage, for it will continue to evolve throughout implementation.

Some of the material included will be common with that of the design document. The inclusion of structure charts, detailed designs and data structure designs is mandatory. However, we must remember that the designer produces *abstract data structures*. So it will be up to the progammers to add *concrete structures* to the manual. An important aid to the maintainers is the *file and data cross-reference*, as mentioned earlier. This too should be included.

Where the new software interfaces with an existing software package or database, the nature of the interface must be described explicitly. Also the details of the testing and integration programme and the results obtained should be included. Once again, this will need to be provided by the staff who conduct the testing programme.

11.3.2 User manual

The user manual will be the key reference for the people who will actually use the system. We would expect such a document to explain the functionality of the software. It should also describe in exhaustive detail the nature of the human/computer interface, the inputs that are acceptable and the outputs that are to be expected.

As humans are only human after all, there should be a complete list of error messages and the corrective action that is required. Finally, if the system incorporates on-line help files, the details of these files and the circumstances in which they may be of assistance should be listed.

If the software is part of a large organizational information system, the user manual may need to take other matters into account. It may be necessary to describe the clerical routines to be adopted in preparing input, the handling of error transactions and the procedures for disposing of output.

11.3.3 User guide

When a system is designed to be operated by user personnel using terminals, then there is an element of training to be considered. One way of tackling this is to provide tutorial material in the form of a user guide. This is the type of material that you probably encountered when you first started using a computer.

Obviously, this could encompass a vast range of activities from general keyboard familiarization to actually entering dummy transactions or attempting exercises. The actual level at which the user guide is pitched will depend on the experience of the trainees, the attitude of the organization towards training and the level of sophistication or otherwise of the new system.

11.4 DOCUMENTATION SUMMARY

In this brief chapter we have tried to convey the nature of the outputs from the design stage. We have tended to use the term *document* freely. But note that nowhere have we implied that any document *must* be printed on paper. Such documents may be and are, increasingly, electronic by nature.

We already mentioned word processing as a means of continually updating the design document. It is but a small step conceptually anyway, to the next stage which is that of the *IPSE, the integrated project support environment.*

An IPSE is a collection of linked computer programs, such as text editors, compilers, debuggers, and so on, which is designed to assist in the development of software. Thus, a designer may sit at a terminal and create detailed designs expressed in PDL, say, as computer files. Come implementation time, programmers may access the designer's files, code them, and test and document the resulting programs.

Documents may, therefore, remain in electronic form for ever. The user guide, for instance, may never be printed on paper. Admittedly, a large document such as the design document itself will be printed at some stage. But it is only likely to be formally issued as such when it is in its final version.

REFERENCES

IEEE (1986) *P1016, Recommended Practice for Software Design Descriptions*, IEEE Computer Society, New York.
Pressman, R. S. (1982) *Software Engineering: a Practitioner's Approach*, McGraw-Hill, London. (2nd edn, 1987)

SUMMARY AND FURTHER READING II

12.1 SUMMARY OF CHAPTERS 6–11

We commenced our discussion of design by placing a realistic limit on the aspirations of the software designer. We pointed out that, as designers, although we might legitimately hope to produce very good designs it was most unlikely that we could create the best possible.

We then proceeded to state that it is only because of constraints and the judicious use of heuristics that design may be accomplished at all. We then saw how, starting from a specification in dataflow diagram form, we could apply a design strategy that would enable an initial design to be produced relatively quickly. We saw also how this first-cut design might be refined into something rather better by the application of the aforesaid heuristics.

We then introduced the notional sequence of detailed design and data structure design but pointed out that, although the former should marginally precede the latter, in practice they are frequently carried out in parallel.

Finally, we looked briefly at the subject of design documentation and ruminated on the content of the constituent documents.

12.2 FURTHER READING

For an erudite treatment of initial design techniques and notations, one can do little better than study the following:

E. Yourdon and L. L. Constantine, *Structured Design: Fundamentals of a Discipline of Computer Program and System Design*, Prentice-Hall, Englewood Cliffs, New Jersey, 1979.

The same ground is covered largely by

M. Page-Jones, *The Practical Guide to Structured System Design*, 2nd edn, Prentice-Hall, Englewood Cliffs, New Jersey, 1988. (1st edn was published by Yourdon Press, 1980.)

The style is less formal and more laid-back than that of Yourdon and Constantine, but nevertheless Page-Jones has plenty to say that is pertinent to the nuts and bolts of design. If, on the other hand, design philosophy is to your taste then the following is strongly recommended:

H. A. Simon, *The New Science of Management Decision*, Harper & Row, London, 1960.

This collection of lectures by Professor Simon may be regarded, perhaps, as being rather ancient. But to our minds the book has plenty to say that is fresh and relevant to anyone who is involved in the design of anything whatever.

For a less than in-depth survey of design methodologies, most of the modern books on software engineering can oblige. One of the better examples of the genre is

R. S. Pressman, *Software Engineering: a Practitioner's Approach*, 2nd edn, McGraw-Hill, London, 1987. (1st edn was 1982.)

There is now a trend towards the use of more formal methods, usually based on set theory, for specification and design. Anyone contemplating making a career in this area will encounter these methods sooner or later. One of the more readable books on this approach is

D. A. Lamb, *Software Engineering: Planning for Change*, Prentice-Hall, Englewood Cliffs, New Jersey, 1988.

For those readers whose role in life is destined to be that of a user but, nevertheless, have a deep interest in all facets of software engineering, the following is recommended:

A. Macro and J. Buxton, *The Craft of Software Engineering*, Addison-Wesley, Wokingham, 1987.

On the whole it is better to avoid any book that has a title that includes the words 'analysis and design' and/or 'information systems', and is liberally illustrated with photographs of computer equipment. Generally, such books are biased towards commercial data processing. In our view this is too narrow a context in which to study software design and it is hoped that the general applicability of our approach to all types of application has been made apparent.

SOLUTIONS TO EXERCISES

Exercise 1.1

Basically, there are three causes which engender the need for intermittent attention to be paid to the software throughout its working life. The first, which was mentioned explicitly in the text, is the presence of errors or 'bugs'. The second, which was implied, is changes to the operating environment in which the software works, and may include hardware or operating systems replacement or enhancement. Any such change may require the modification of applications software. The final cause, so far unmentioned, is environmental change. By this we mean alterations to the organization or mechanism that the software is serving. For instance, if the software provides control information to a company, then a change in management personnel (who may well have different ideas on the information that they require) can lead to the need for comprehensive changes to the system. Similarly, real-time software may need to be changed if new sensing equipment is incorporated in the controlled system.

Exercise 2.1

The answer to this question falls naturally into two parts. First, there is the problem of determining what the behaviour is, and there are a number of techniques, obvious and less-obvious, for doing this: inspection of procedure manuals, observation, interviewing, questionnaires, sampling. Procedure manuals should be the most fruitful source of information about an existing system and their perusal is essential. Unfortunately, they frequently suffer from a serious drawback: they are out of date. Perhaps changes have been made to the system which have not been recorded because of oversight, lack of time or some similar cause. They are also, on the whole, tedious to read and as they depend largely on natural language description, they tend to contain ambiguities. For these reasons, the study of manuals must be backed up by observing what is going on and by interviewing the staff involved.

Needless to say, both of these activities must be conducted with care and the latter, particularly, is difficult to carry out effectively unless the analyst is very experienced or has received appropriate training. Occasionally, the analyst will feel that the use of a questionnaire is the only way of discovering some necessary information. The analyst should be invited to think again. Great skill is required to avoid ambiguity and confusion so that this approach is only worth while if a large number of respondents or many remote locations are involved. Where high volumes of documents, transactions or activities are concerned it may not be practical to investigate the total number. In these circumstances, the investigation must be confined to a sample. Clearly, bias in the sample must be avoided and the statistical significance must be understood. This may require specialist advice.

The second part of the answer relates to the recording of behaviour once it is determined. This will require the use of appropriate notations. An introduction to these notations forms a substantial part of the subject matter of Chapter 3.

Exercise 2.2

There are a number of possible answers to this question and they mainly relate to the expectations of the user. Some of the most important, in our view, we can list:

Economy, Reliability, Maintainability, Robustness, Integrity, Security

In other words, what the user would really like is a system that is cheap to develop and run, never breaks down, is easy to maintain, can handle large variations in volumes of transactions, and whose programs and data are impervious to corruption or destruction both accidentally and deliberately. As many of these properties are mutually exclusive, it is apparent that the user will be unlucky. The designer has to acquire some feeling for how the user rates these properties, and then select the design accordingly. This involves the art of *trading off*. For instance, faced with the choice between the highly maintainable system A and the very reliable system B, the designer must be in the position to decide how much reliability the user is prepared to sacrifice to gain so much maintainability — and vice versa.

Exercise 2.3

The deceptively obvious approach is to choose an appropriate moment at which to stop the old system and introduce the new. Some applications do lend themselves to this approach, particularly if the changeover point is a natural one. As an example we can take accounting systems, for a natural break is often provided by the end of the financial year. Even so, the break is normally a small one, a few hours at most, before the application has to be working again. Consequently, unless the system is small and simple, it may not be possible to sort out any teething problems before business starts again.

The above approach becomes even less attractive if the application in question is large, complex and essential to health or personal safety. Real-time systems for air traffic control or chemical plant monitoring may come into this class. For these, and many other applications, alternative strategies have to be employed. These fall into one of two main categories.

The first of these is *parallel running*. As the name implies, the old and the new systems are run in parallel and the outputs compared. After the new system has settled down and is judged to be working correctly, the old system is terminated. Interestingly, a period of parallel running will often reveal faults in the old system that nobody knew existed. This, of course, acts like a shot in the arm for the developers of the new system who, by this stage of the life cycle, are probably fed up with the whole thing and thinking of early retirement.

The second type of strategy is often referred to as *pilot running* or *incremental cut over*. The system is notionally partitioned so that it may be converted in parts. The philosophy is that even if a small section of the application is having problems with a new system, the majority of functions will be unaffected. One might imagine for instance that a new payroll scheme might be implemented initially for one department. Alternatively, a new airline reservations scheme might be applied to only one route. Once the pilot system is running correctly then other parts may be included progressively into the scheme until the whole application has been taken over.

Exercise 3.1

(a) We would expect the motorist to view the filling station as just that, i.e., an establishment where the fuel tank may be replenished, the oil, water and tyres checked and, if very lucky, the windscreen cleaned.

(b) The owner of the fast food chain may view it as a handy piece of real estate, entirely suitable for demolition and the subsequent erection of a new outlet for Jellied Eelburgers plc. Although not of immediate relevance, it is worth noting that as different individuals take different views of systems, the criteria by which they judge or rank them will also vary. This is entirely consistent with our discussion of Exercise 2.2, where the properties that we listed were probably at variance with your own selection.

Exercise 3.2

Careful examination of the user requirements indicates that only two other statements are truly functional: (c) and (f). The first of these, (c), gives some idea as to how the commitment information is to be assembled and summarized. The latter indicates that for the benefit of managers, some manipulation of data and subsequent reporting will be necessary. You may feel inclined to quibble with this answer, and this is to be expected at this stage. However, by the end of this chapter, when the other categories of requirement will have been defined, the correctness of this solution should be more apparent.

Exercise 3.3

Constraints are indicated by statements (d) and (g). Statement (d) indicates an upper limit on the total size of the purchase commitments files. We do not know, but we can presume that this is something to do with the amount of disk storage, or similar media, available for the application. For whatever reason, the designer is instructed that a class of designs, i.e., all those requiring more than 4 megabytes of file space, are unacceptable. On the other hand, (g) tells the developers that certain standards must be applied in developing software. All designs failing to meet those standards must be rejected.

Exercise 3.4

There is one, (e). This indicates that the user is probably suffering. The organization is having to maintain a number of existing programs and it is costing an arm and a leg. Therefore, the user is asking for highly modular, maintainable software, just the sort of software, in fact, that we shall be designing in a later chapter.

Exercise 3.5

The first stage of the procedure calls for the identification and extraction of any design decisions. There is only one statement of this kind in the document, statement 9. This is an explicit attempt to influence the nature of the ultimate design. It is expressing *how* the job is to be done. Therefore, it is a case for the exercise of persuasion in order to have the statement withdrawn. The next stage is to identify the design objectives. There is only one. This is statement 5 wherein the user is expressing a preference for a system that uses little main memory at the expense, perhaps, of processing speed. Following from this the non-functional requirements are extracted. Statements 2, 3 and 4 come into this category for they constrain the design in terms of programming language, input format and program size. Statement 6 is a little marginal. It is possible to argue that it is both functional and non-functional, but as it has implications for memory constraints it is probably better to regard it as the latter. This leaves statements 1, 7 and 8 as functional requirements. Statement 1 is very general. It is statements 7 and 8 that will provide the main impetus to the requirements analysis procedures.

Exercise 3.6

In this case there are three that we have been informed about. One is the flow of signals from the strain gauges placed on objects in the wind tunnel. Another is the sequence of symbolic names with associated pressure gauge numbers to be input by the operator. Finally, there is the item, AVERAGE PERIOD. This is to be entered by the operator also. In this case, the functional requirements are rather more specific than in the purchase commitments document, so that the inputs we have identified are probably exhaustive. This may not be so as far as outputs are concerned, as we shall see later.

Exercise 3.7

The interpretation here is that either flow I9 or flow I12 will be transformed by T10 into flow I13. I13, in its turn, will be transformed by T11 into flows I15 and I16.

Exercise 3.8

The level 0 DFD is displayed in Fig. E1.

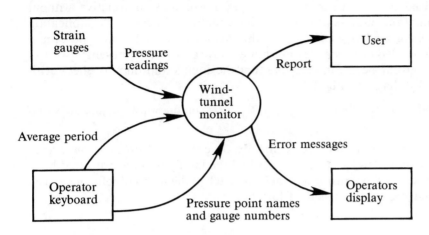

Figure E1 Level 0 DFD for the wind-tunnel monitoring system.

The diagram is compiled entirely on the basis of the user requirement document, Fig. 3.3, with one exception. With manual input from the operator keyboard, there is always a possibility of error, a point that was made about input generally, in the main text. Consequently, a flow of error messages to the operator display is incorporated in the diagram. This, of course, entails the inclusion of the operator display as a sink, the appropriate square symbol being used for this purpose.

Exercise 3.9

This is probably best approached in the following fashion. It is apparent that there is a natural partition in the function of the software. First, there is a part of the system that is involved with manual input via the operator keyboard. Second, there is a part that is concerned with the input, processing and output of pressure readings. If we assign a transform to each of these functions then we arrive at a DFD as shown in Fig. E2.

The linkage between the two transforms is provided by two information flows: *valid average period* and *pressure point names and gauge numbers*. We could perhaps reason that we had refined the system far enough to give us level 1. After all, this is to about the same level of detail as level 1 of the purchase commitments system, Fig. 3.9. However, the user requirement document is more explicit in this case and we are justified in attempting a little further refinement. Certain aspects of the user requirements provides clues as to the ultimate form of the level 1 diagram. This occurs most noticeably in connection with time. For instance, the series of pressure point names/gauge numbers is input at the beginning of the experiment but is not required until the end. This implies the need for a file or store. Similarly, averages of pressure readings are derived throughout the experiment but, again, are not used until the end. Thus a case is made for another store. Other clues are the need to decode the pressure reading signals, the need to provide validity checks if error messages are to be generated, and so on. All these points, and others, lead us to the type of level 1 DFD displayed in Fig. E3.

We have arrived at a seven-transform diagram which is informative without reaching the point of incomprehensibility. We have maintained clarity by duplicating the file *pressure point names/gauge numbers* and thus avoided the need to cross flow lines. (Note that this is intended to be *one* file only, but we have chosen to represent it twice as a diagrammatic convenience.) Finally, note that the inputs and outputs check with those for the level 0 diagram, Fig. E1.

Exercise 3.10

The behaviour of the non-primitives is already described in terms of lower-level transforms, information flows and stores. So, of all the family of transforms that have been identified, it is only the transforms that have reached the limits of refinement, i.e., the primitives, that need to be specified further.

Exercise 3.11

A possible answer to this exercise is shown in Fig. E4.

We have varied the notation a little here but we have not introduced any new features. We have tried to practise what we preach to the extent of inventing a process ID and process name. When illustrated in this way the process can easily be seen to consist of three nested loops with a decision construct located in the innermost. In this case, most certainly, the structured English version, in terms of clarity, seems to outshine the natural language version of the problem statement.

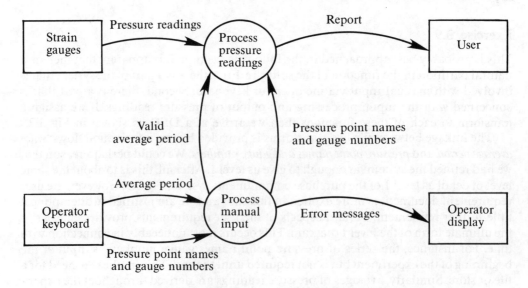

Figure E2 Initial partitioning of the level 0 DFD for the wind-tunnel monitoring system.

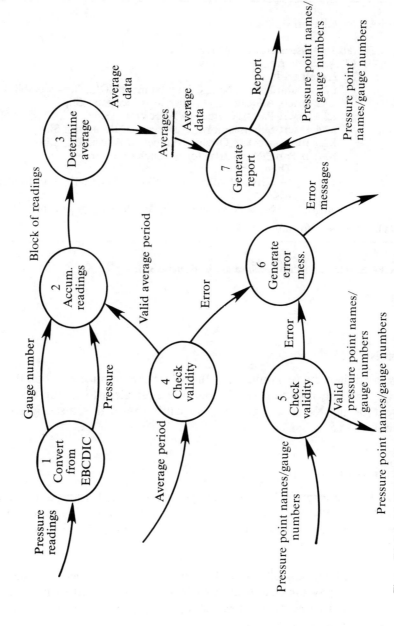

Figure E3 Level 1 DFD for the wind-tunnel monitoring system.

PROCESS ID: WO 7.3   PROCESS NAME: Works Order Processing

REPEAT for all Works__Orders

   1 For all sub-assemblies on Works__Order
      1.1 Access Parts__List
      1.2 For all parts
          1.2.1 Multiply Number__Off by Number__Of__Sub-assemblies-Required
          1.2.2 Insert Allocated__Number in Allocation__Slip
          1.2.3 Insert Part__Number in Allocation__Slip
          1.2.4 Insert Sub-assembly__Number in Allocation__Slip
          1.2.5 Insert Works__Order__Number in Allocation__Slip
          1.2.6 If Part__Number is for a bought-out part
                Then,
                    Forward Allocation__Slip to Material Control Dept
                Else,
                    Send Allocation__Slip to Data Entry Section

UNTIL there are no more Works__Orders

Figure E4 Structured English specification in Exercise 3.11.

Exercise 3.12

Translated literally we would show this using the iteration symbol, thus: $0\{X\}1$. Alternatively, we can note that this is logically equivalent to saying that either one X is present or no Xs at all. So that we can express this also by using the option symbol, (X).

Exercise 3.13

We were quite surprised (and perhaps you were too) at the amount of information on a cheque completed for payment. In general terms, and using one of our own cheque books as a basis, it seems as though an adequate definition would be the following:

cheque = 2{bank name}2 + bank address + 2{bank code}2 + date
           + payee name + amount in words + amount in numerals
           + 1{name of account holder} + 1{signature} + cheque number
           + account number

The above is largely self-explanatory. The only items that may require explanation are *bank name* and *bank code*. The definition indicates that both of these items occur precisely twice.

Exercise 3.14

The definition requires the straightforward application of the given symbols and can be expressed in one line:

personnel = 3000{name + address + NI number + (tax code)}5000

We merely use the iteration symbol (with constraints) to indicate that the file consists of a number of records and define the record format in terms of the data items therein.

Exercise 7.1

In the context of the adding problem only an infinitesimal fraction of the possible designs is actually considered. There is a very high probability, therefore, that the best design is not among them. In fact, it is highly unlikely that any of the best thousand or even million is among them. They, like the baby, have been thrown out with the bath water. But if the heuristic is a good one, the designer should be left with a very good design, and this is the best that any designer can hope for.

Exercise 7.2

The calculation is now quite mechanical. We merely evaluate expression (2) for each design, thus obtaining a *value* for each design, $V(X)$, $V(Y)$ and $V(Z)$, respectively. This is accomplished in the following way. For each design, read off the value from the corresponding value function for each attribute. Multiply each value by the appropriate c factor and sum the products. The design with the highest V value is regarded as the best, as follows:

Design X Let value of design X be represented by $V(X)$.
$V(X) = (0.2 \times 100) + (0.5 \times 0) + (0.3 \times 75) = 20 + 0 + 22.5 = 42.5$
Design Y Let value of design Y be represented by $V(Y)$.
$V(Y) = (0.2 \times 16) + (0.5 \times 25) + (0.3 \times 100) = 3.2 + 12.5 + 30 = 45.7$
Design Z Let value of design Z be represented by $V(Z)$.
$V(Z) = (0.2 \times 0) + (0.5 \times 100) + (0.3 \times 0) = 0 + 50 + 0 = 50$

Application of the value function thus selects Z, with $V(Z)$ equal to 50, as the preferred design.

Exercise 7.3

The only difference now is that the weighting factors must be changed. Bearing in mind that the three weighting constants must sum to unity, we arrive at values of $c1 = 0.4, c2 = 0.2, c3 = 0.4$. Using the same approach as before:

$V(X) = (0.4 \times 100) + (0.2 \times 0) + (0.4 \times 75) = 70$
$V(Y) = (0.4 \times 16) + (0.2 \times 25) + (0.4 \times 100) = 51.4$
$V(Z) = (0.4 \times 0) + (0.2 \times 100) + (0.4 \times 0) = 20$

It may be seen that application of the same value functions, but with different weightings, results in the selection of design *X*.

Exercise 8.1

If we can take the module identifiers at their face value then it appears that EXECU-TIVE is concerned with reading blocks which consist of a number of temperature readings, calculating the average of the readings and printing this average value. To this end, EXECUTIVE is able to call READBLOCK which passes a block of temperatures or an end-of-file flag. EXECUTIVE may also call another module, FINDAV, passing to it a block of temperatures. FINDAV may in turn call CALCAV, passing on the block of temperatures and receiving back a value for average temperature. FINDAV may then call PRINTAV and pass the average temperature to it. PRINTAV will then print the average temperature.

Exercise 8.2

Record types that are parameters to more than one module, downward-travelling flags, global data areas and, most important of all, referencing the inside of other modules, should all be avoided if at all possible.

Exercise 8.3

There is plenty of scope for argument here. Although on the face of it the most complex, we think we would vote for C as being the most cohesive of the four. It is carrying out the whole of one function and no parts of any other. It is a toss up between B and D for the number two slot. They both have two minor functions to perform but B, dealing as it does with initialization, might be regarded as exhibiting temporal cohesion. If we were feeling generous we might decide that D seems to be sequentially cohesive and give it the edge over B. The remaining module, A, is a curious mish-mash. It calculates tax, but not any other deductions that are always involved in net pay calculations. We do not think we would try and put a name to it but it does not sound very cohesive to us, so we declare it to be the back marker.

Exercise 8.4

The view of A taken by S is that it is an afferent module. On demand, it is required to deliver *y* and that is all. A, as seen by T, is the boss, a coordinate module. On demand, T does as it is told and provides data item *x* to A. A's view of B is that it is a transform module. The provision of *x* to B results in the conversion into, and the return of *y*. The module S has no view of B whatever. In fact, it does not even know of B's existence. If it *does* know of B, then A is less than a black box and the design is suspect.

Exercise 8.5

The basic difficulty with this exercise lies with the isolation of the central transforms.

There are many candidates: *Calculate xs speed, Convert to rpm, Calculate fuel consumption* and *Calculate gph*. A persuasive case could probably be made for many combinations of these, if we set our minds to it.

However, we must make a start somewhere, so we are going to regard flows with the following symbolic names as the highest levels of afferent data that are furthest from physical input: c, f and h. Similarly, we shall regard d, g and i as the highest levels of efferent data that are furthest removed from physical output. If these flows are bisected and the bisections are joined, then we arrive at Fig. E5.

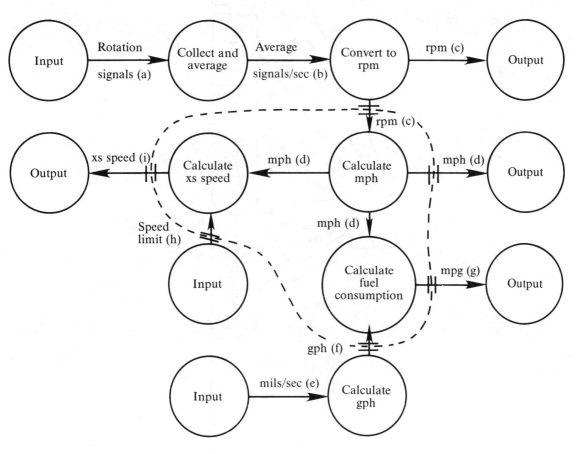

Figure E5 Isolation of central transforms.

From Fig. E5 we can see that our choice of highest-level afferent and efferent flows has led to the selection of *Calculate xs speed, Calculate mph* and *Calculate fuel consumption* as the central transforms. It is now a simple matter to conduct the first level factoring and the result is shown in Fig. E6.

148

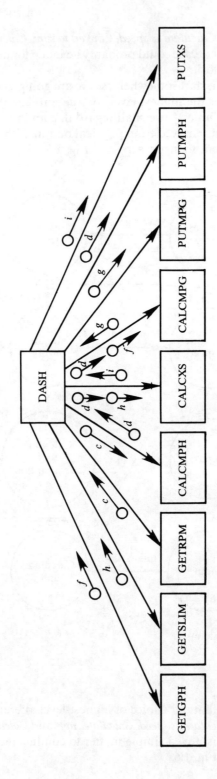

Figure E6 First level factoring of DASH.

We have named a main module DASH. For each afferent data item feeding a central transform a subordinate module has been specified: GETRPH, GETSLIM and GETRPM. Similarly, we have specified PUTMPG, PUTMPH and PUTXS as subordinate efferent modules. Finally, we have specified subordinate transform modules for each of the central transforms: CALCMPH, CALCXS and CALCMPG.

We now have to face up to factoring the afferent, efferent and transform branches. In fact, there are only two first level modules where further factoring is necessary, GETGPH and GETRPM. So we follow the standard factoring procedure for these two modules and arrive at Fig. E7.

We could regard the initial design as complete if it were not for one thing. We have omitted to take account of the output to the rev. counter. It has escaped our attention so far because this is not an efferent flow emerging from a central transform. In order to accommodate this feature of the specification we now have to deploy our skills as designers, for our design strategy cannot help us any more.

Clearly, we need another module, named PUTRPM, say, and there are at least three places where we could attach it. The obvious place is to make it a subordinate efferent module to DASH. It would then take its place side-by-side with the other modules that drive the dashboard display. However, for reasons which will have to await the study of Sec. 8.6, this would not be regarded as very smart. In fact, the design as it stands at the moment is not all that outstanding and we shall refer back to it in Exercise 8.7.

For the moment, let us just say that we would like the design to reflect more closely the shape of the problem that we are trying to solve. In the DFD the rev. counter is driven directly by the output from the transform *Convert to rpm*, so we could make PUTRPM subordinate to CONVRPM. However, this complicates a simple and potentially useful little transform module. It might be better, therefore, to make PUTRPM subordinate to GETRPM as this latter module is already carrying out a managerial role. So that is what we shall do. Accordingly, we end up with a second version of the structure chart for DASH and this is shown as Fig. E8.

We have ended up with a first-cut design that is probably adequate. But we must emphasize that the isolation of a different set of transforms could result in a totally different but, as far as we can tell, equally acceptable solution. If you have some time to spare you might like to experiment by varying the selection of central transforms and comparing your resulting designs with the above.

Exercise 8.6

See Fig. E9.

Exercise 8.7

Let us commence this exercise by considering the name of the system—COMPUTE NET PAY. To the impartial observer the top module does just that. However, we know from Fig. 8.27 that there are three classes of worker, hourly, salaried and casual, involved. So it seems sensible for COMPUTE NET PAY to delegate the task to three subordinate modules, each one being charged with calculating net pay for a particular worker class. We arrive very quickly at the first part of the new design as shown in Fig. E10.

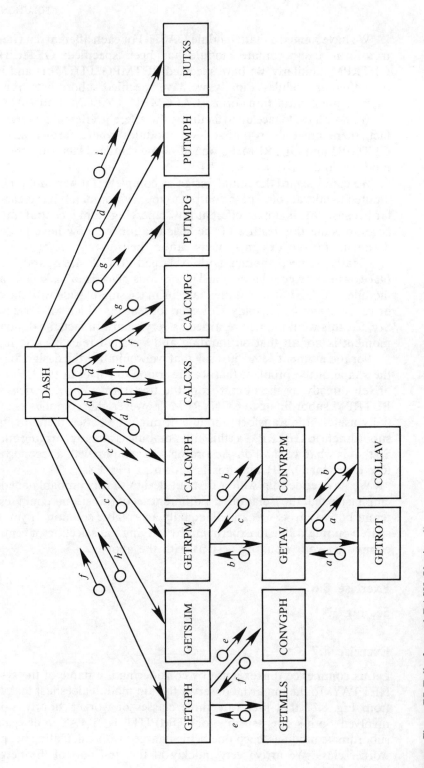

Figure E.7 Fully factored DASH (Version 1).

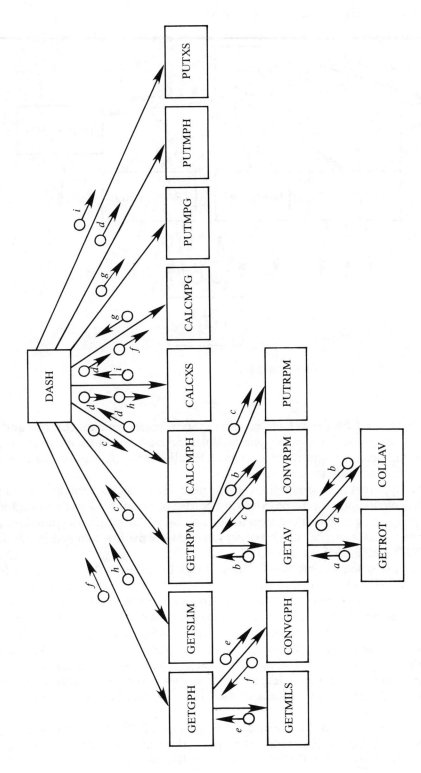

Figure E8 Fully factored DASH (Version 2).

151

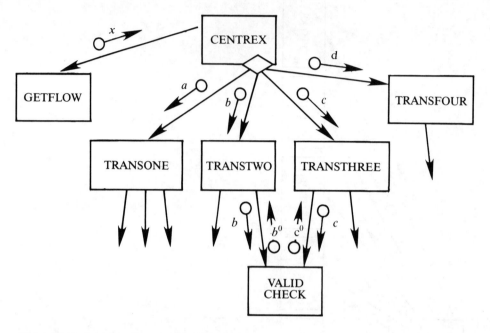

Figure E9 Revised structure chart for CENTREX.

COMPUTE NET PAY now has four direct subordinates which it controls and co-ordinates. To the three *Calculate net pay* modules we have added the module *Get pay data*. So the implication is that the master module calls for pay data and dispatches it to the appropriate subordinate for processing.

Now it is apparent from the original structure chart that the computation of net pay involves the calculation of gross pay (fees in the case of casual workers), calculation of the appropriate tax and the calculation of deductions. All three of these functions can be made subordinate to the calculation of net pay and we arrive at a complete partitioning of COMPUTE NET PAY, as in Fig. E11.

We should like you to note two features of this final design. First of all, we have achieved a savage reduction in the fan-out of COMPUTE NET PAY. This is what we set out to do and we would expect the master module to be more cohesive as a result. The second point is that we took note of the fact that only one *Schedule E tax* module and only one *Normal deductions* module appeared in the original chart, Fig. 8.27. We can assume with reasonable safety, therefore, that these modules may be used for calculating both *Hourly net pay* and *Salaried net pay*. This has enabled us to build in some extra fan-in into the structure. High fan-in, like a high-fibre diet, is generally regarded as a good thing, but for a slightly more complete discussion on this matter you should read Sec. 8.6.3.

Finally, let us return briefly to Exercise 8.5 and Figs E5, E6 and E7. With hindsight we can now see that it was not modesty that led to our statement that 'the design . . . is not all that outstanding.' For DASH has been saddled with a fan-out of nine, and this

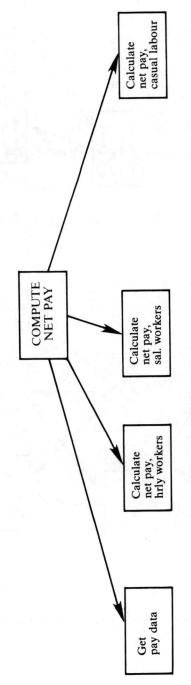

Figure E10 First level partitioning of COMPUTE NET PAY.

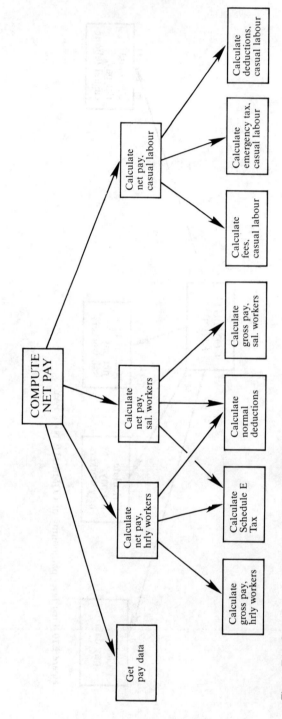

Figure E11 Complete partitioning of COMPUTE NET PAY.

explains our reluctance to increase the burden on DASH by imposing yet another direct subordinate, PUTRPM. In accordance with the philosophy outlined in Sec. 8.6.2, DASH is a candidate for critical examination.

If we decided that a reduction in the fan-out of DASH was highly desirable, we could most easily achieve this by inserting intermediate-level modules in the afferent and efferent branches. We would then have a structure, the first level of which would be as in Fig. E12.

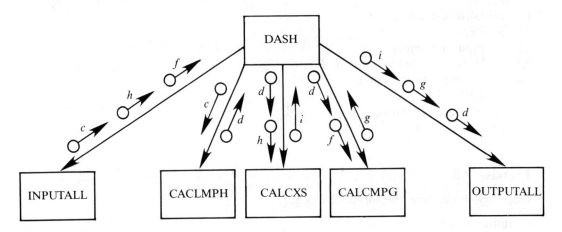

Figure E12 DASH with intermediate afferent and efferent modules.

We have reduced the fan-out of DASH sure enough but we would need to be sure that INPUTALL and OUTPUTALL are at least *temporally cohesive* for us to be convinced that we have really improved the structure. Unless the inputs, c, h and f, on the one hand, and the outputs, i, g and d, on the other, are related in time, then we might be inserting two logically cohesive modules into the structure. The cure might be worse than the ailment.

As far as we are concerned, this particular design decision must go by default for we do not have enough information on which to base a choice. But remember that, fairly frequently, the alternatives to an excessively large fan-out are even less desirable than the fan-out itself. So you just have to learn to live with it.

Exercise 9.1

The only extra information that we have relates to Statement 2 and so we decompose this by using a CASE construct:

```
1     obtain a command
2.1   CASE command OF
2.3      'PRINT': print the file
2.3      'DELETE': remove all flight records from the file
2.4      'UPDATE': update a flight record
2.5   END_CASE
```

Exercise 9.2

We may show the top-level design in the following fashion:

1 initialize a count of zero
2 input a series of numbers and count the positive ones
3 print the count

We can transform this into a more useful representation by refining step 2:

```
1    initialize a count of zero
2.1  REPEAT
2.2      input a number
2.3      IF the number is positive THEN
2.4          add 1 to the count
2.5      END_IF
2.6  UNTIL the last number is processed
3    print the count
```

Exercise 9.3

Once again we show the top-level design:

1 initialize a count of zero
2 obtain messages, count the ones for London and add all messages to the queue
3 print the count

By the usual refinement process we end with the detailed design:

```
1    initialize a count of zero
2.1  WHILE there are messages to be added DO
2.2      obtain a message
2.3      IF the message is for London THEN
2.4          increment the count
2.5      END_IF
2.6      add the message to the queue
2.7  END_WHILE
3    print the count
```

Exercise 9.4

On the basis that we wish to calculate the average for each successive 100 readings, and that the average of the whole 1000 readings will be regarded as the *average of the averages*, we can rapidly identify the top level of our detailed design as follows:

1 zeroize an accumulator for the averages of each 100 readings
2 calculate, accumulate and print the average of each 100 readings
3 calculate average of 1000 readings
4 print average of 1000 readings

5   set difference equal to the difference between the average of 1000 readings and 98.4

All that is required now is to apply step-wise refinement to 2, and cloak the whole thing in more formal language. We thus arrived at the final detailed design:

```
MODULE patientmonitor (difference)
1     set average100sum to zero
2.1       FOR counter10 FROM 1 to 10 DO
2.2           set sum100 to zero
2.3.1             FOR counter100 FROM 1 TO 100 DO
2.3.2                 CALL getatemp (temp)
2.3.3                     add temp to sum100
2.3.4             ENDFOR
2.4           set average100 to sum100 divided by 100
2.5           add average100 to average100sum
2.6           print out average100
2.7       ENDFOR
3     set average1000 to average100sum divided by 10
4     print out average1000
5     set difference equal to the difference between average1000 and 98.4
END_MODULE
```

As may be seen, this design is based on nested FOR constructs embedded in a sequence.

Exercise 9.5

You probably found this exercise tedious rather than difficult, the point being that although Fig. 9.15 appears to include four decisions, two of them are repetition constructs. Consequently, the DSD version appears as in Fig. E13.

This exercise gives some insight into the travails of a programmer, programming in a modern structured language, who is required to work from a flowchart. For his or her problems will be exactly the same as the ones that you experienced in tackling this problem.

Exercise 10.1

Model (a) requires less space but is less efficient in terms of dealing with additions and deletions.

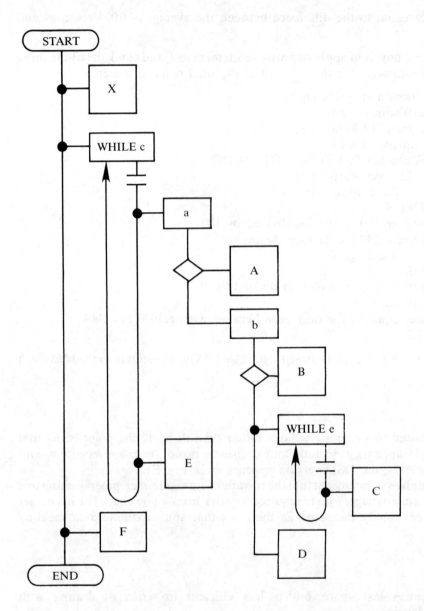

Figure E13 Flowchart of Fig. 9.15 converted into a DSD (adapted from BS 6224: 1987).

INDEX

Abstract data, 120
Afferent flow, 70
Afferent module, 70
Aggregate identifier, 57
Annotation, use of, in DSD, 114–117

Black box, 60
Boundary element, 57
Bubble chart (*see* Dataflow diagrams)

Central transforms, 70, 72–75
Cohesion, 61, 64, 82
    coincidental, 64
    communicational, 66
    functional, 68
    logical, 65
    ordinal ranking of, 64
    procedural, 65
    sequential, 67
    temporal, 65
Combinatorial explosion, 43
Composite design, 55
Conceptual modelling, 121–124
Concrete data, 120
Consistency, 10
Constraints, 14, 45–46
Conversion, 8
Coordinate module, 71
Costs:
    developments, 10
    total life-cycle, 8
Coupling, 61, 82
    common, 62
    content, 61
    control, 62
    data, 62

ordinal ranking of, 61
    pathological, 61
    stamp, 62
Cut-over (*see* Conversion)

Data couple, 59
Data dictionary, 30–32
    definition notation, 30
    supplementary information, 32
    treatment of aliases, 32
Data structure:
    array, 120
    composite, 121
    design, 56, 119
    dynamic, 120
    record, 120
    sequence, 120
    static, 120
    tree, 120
Dataflow diagrams, 19
    elements of, 19
    imposing system boundary on, 20–21
    internal consistency of, 24
    level 0, 23–24
    level 1, 24–25
    level 2, 3, etc., 25–26
    levelled set of, 25
    notation, 19–20
    procedural annotation of, 21–22
    step-wise refinement of, 24
Debugging, 8
Decision:
    representation in DSD, 104–109
    representation in PDL, 97–98
Decision-making, 42
Decision tables, 28
Decision tree, 28

159